Military Of The Republic Of China, including: Republic Of China Armed Forces, Whampoa Military Academy, National Revolutionary Army, Republic Of China Military Academy, Republic Of China And Weapons Of Mass Destruction, Wuchih Mountain Military Cemetery

Hephaestus Books

Contents

Articles

Republic of China Armed Forces

Republic of China Armed Forces

Republic of China Armed Forces 中華民國國軍	
ROCN La Fayette class frigate patrolling the territorial waters near Taiwan.	
Service branches	Republic of China Army Republic of China Navy Republic of China Air Force Republic of China Military Police
Headquarters	Taipei, Republic of China
Leadership	
Commander-in-Chief	ROC President Ma Ying-jeou
Minister of National Defence	Gao Hua-Jhu
Chief of the General Staff	General Huo Sho-yeh
Manpower	
Military age	19 - 40 years of age
Conscription	1 year compulsory military services for male citizens between the age of 19 and 40
Available for military service	5,883,828, age 15-40 (2005 est.)
Fit for military service	4,749,537, age 15-40 (2005 est.)

Reaching military age annually	174,173 (2005 est.)
Active personnel	290,000 (ranked 16th)
Reserve personnel	1,675,000
Expenditures	
Budget	$10.5 billion (2008 est.) (ranked 20th)
Percent of GDP	2.5 (2008 est.)
Industry	
Domestic suppliers	Aerospace Industrial Development Corporation, Chungshan Institute of Science and Technology, CSBC Corporation, Taiwan, 205th Armory
Foreign suppliers	United States France Germany United Kingdom(BAE)
Related articles	
Ranks	Republic of China Armed Forces rank insignia

Until the 1970s, the military's primary mission was to retake mainland China from the Chinese communist People's Republic of China (PRC) through the Project National Glory. The military's current foremost mission is the defence of the islands of Taiwan, Penghu, Kinmen, Matsu against a possible military invasion by the People's Liberation Army of the People's Republic of China, which is seen as the predominant threat to the ROC in the ongoing dispute over the political status of Taiwan.

Personnel

See also: Conscription in the Republic of China

The ROC's armed forces number approximately 300,000, and reserves reportedly total 3,870,000. Conscription remains universal for qualified males reaching age 18. Force streamlining programs under way since 1997 are combining redundant institutions and steadily reducing the military to 270,000 personnel by 2012. However, even then there would be compulsory basic training for all males reaching 18. As the size of the force decreases, the ROC intends to gradually expand the number of volunteer soldiers with the eventual goal of forming an all volunteer career force.

The ROC military's officer corps is generally viewed as being competent, capable, technically proficient, displaying a high degree of professionalism. However, as a whole, the culture in the officer corps tends to be very cautious and conservative. The military also faces difficulties in the recruitment and retention of junior officers and NCO's due to competition with the private sector. There are, however, plans to make it a volunteer armed forces.

Because of the historical legacy having once controlled mainland China, the army has traditionally been the most important of the ROC's armed forces, although this has declined in recent years with the realization that the traditional army's role in defending against a PRC invasion is limited. As a result, recent force modernization programs have resulted in the reorganization of the Army into smaller units that will act as fast mobile reserve troops to counterattack landings made by PLA (People's Liberation Army) forces. For the same reason, more emphasis is being placed on the development of the Navy and Air Force, in order to fend off attacks in the Taiwan Strait, away from Taiwan proper.

Organization

Military branches and structure

The following service commands are directly subordinate to the General Staff, headed by the Chief of the General Staff, which answers to the Minister of Defense and the ROC President:

- **Republic of China Army** (ROCA)
- **Republic of China Navy** (ROCN)
    - **Republic of China Marine Corps** (ROCMC)
- **Republic of China Air Force** (ROCAF)
- **Republic of China Military Police** (ROCMP)

The Coast Guard Administration was created in 2001 from related police and military units and is administered by the Executive Yuan and may be incorporated as a military branch during times of emergency but for the most part remains under civilian control.

Arms purchases and weapons development

Acquisitions over the next several years will emphasize modern C^4ISR equipment that will vastly improve communications and data-sharing among services. These and other planned acquisitions will gradually shift the island's strategic emphasis to offshore engagement of invading PRC forces. It is hoped that this will serve to reduce civilian casualties and damage to infrastructure in the event of armed conflict.

The ROC's armed forces are equipped with weapons obtained primarily from the United States, examples being 150 F-16A/B Block-20 MLU fighters, 6 E-2 Hawkeyes, licensed produced *Oliver Hazard Perry*-class frigates, 63 AH-1W attack helos, 39 OH-58D scout helos and 3 batteries of Patriot PAC-II SAMs.

The ROC has also procured two Hai Lung class class submarines from the Netherlands and 60 Mirage 2000-5Di/Ei fighters from France together with six French La Fayette stealth frigates. The ROC also has four German made minesweepers that were bought under guise of civilian use.

In 2001, the United States approved the sale of a number of weapons systems, including the sale of eight diesel submarines, six Patriot PAC-3 SAMs and 12 P-3C Orion maritime patrol aircraft. Out of the items authorised, the ROC currently has four *Kidd*-class destroyers, M109A5 units, two additional E-2C Hawkeyes 2000 and nine CH-47SD Chinook heavy transport helicopters in service, with the 12 P-3C and 3 PAC-3 batteries being funded. It is unclear if or when the balance of the equipment will be supplied. The delivery of diesel submarines in particular is doubtful, as the United States does not manufacture diesel submarines.

The military budget for 2007 (passed 16 June) included funds for the procurement of 12 P-3C Orion patrol aircraft, 66 F-16 C/D Block 52 fighters, the upgrade of existing PAC-2 batteries to PAC-3 standard and a feasibility study into the planned purchase of conventionally-powered submarines offered by the US way back in 2001.

In July 2007 it was reported that the ROC Army would request the purchase of 30 AH-64D II Apache attack helicopters from in the 2008 defence budget. The United Daily News reported that as many as 90 UH-60 Black Hawk helicopters would also be ordered to replace the UH-1Hs currently in service.

During August, the ROC requested 60 AGM-84L Harpoon Block II missiles, 2 Harpoon guidance control units, 30 Harpoon containers, 30 Harpoon extended air-launch lugs, 50 Harpoon upgrade kits from AGM-84G to AGM-84L configuration and other related elements of logistics and program support, the total value being $125 million. The United States government indicated its approval of the order with notification to the United States Congress of the potential sale.

In mid September 2007, the Pentagon notified the U.S. Congress of P-3C Orion order, which included 12 Orions and three "spare aircraft", along with an order for 144 SM-2 Block IIIA missiles. The total value of the 12 P-3C Orions were estimated at around $1.96 billion and $272 million for the 144 SM-2 missiles. A contract was awarded to Lockheed Martin to refurbish the 12 P-3C Orion aircraft for the ROC on March 3, 2009, with deliveries to start in 2012.

In mid November 2007, the Pentagon notified the US Congress about a possible sale to upgrade the ROC's existing 3 Patriot missile batteries to the PAC-3 standard. The total value of the upgrade could be as much as $939 million. So far 1 battery had finished upgrade and sent back to the ROC, while the contract to upgrade second battery had been announced.

The US government announced on the 3rd of October that it planned to sell $6.5 billion dollars worth of arms to the ROC ending the freeze of arms sales to the ROC. The plans include $2.5 billion dollars worth of 30 AH-64D Block III Apache Longbow attack helicopters with night-vision sensors, radar, 174 Stinger Block I air-to-air missiles and 1000 AGM-114L Hellfire missiles. Additionally it will include the sale of PAC-3 missiles (330), 4 missile batteries, radar sets, ground stations and other equipment valued up to $3.1 billion. 4 E-2T aircraft upgrade to E-2C Hawkeye 2000 will also be included worth up to $250 million. $200 million worth of sub launched Harpoon Block II missiles (32) will also be available for sale, $334 million worth of various aircraft spare parts and 182 Javelin missiles, with 20 Javelin command launchers.

However, not included in the arms sale were new F-16 C/D fighters, the feasibility study for diesel-electric submarines or UH-60 Black Hawk helicopters. The White House had declined to sell 66 F-16C/D fighter planes as US Pacific Command has felt no need for advanced arms to be sold to the ROC.

The military has also stressed military "self-reliance", which has led to the growth of indigenous military production, producing items such as the ROC's Indigenous Defense Fighter, the RT-2000 M270 Multiple Launch Rocket System, Clouded Leopard Armoured Vehicle, the Sky Bow I and Sky Bow II SAMs and Hsiung Feng series of anti-ship missiles. The ROC's efforts at arms purchases have consistently been opposed by the People's Republic of China (PRC). The PRC has also consistently attempted to block co-operation between the ROC military and those of other countries.

On January 28, 2010, ROCAF received first batch of new TC-2(V) BVR missiles ordered from CSIST. Believe to have new radar seeker and improved performance from the original missile entered service over 10 years ago.

On January 29, 2010, the US government announced 5 notifications to US Congress for arms sales to the ROC including 2 Osprey class mine hunters for $105 million (USD), 25 Link 16 terminals on ships for $340 million, 10 ship and 2 air launched Harpoon L/II for $37 million, 60 UH-60Ms and other related items for $3.1 billion, and 3 PAC-3 batteries with 26 launchers and 114 PAC-3 missiles for $2.81 Billion.

On February 3, 2010, it was announced at Singapore Airshow that ROCAF had signed contract for 3 EC-225 SAR(Search-And-Rescue) helicopters that was award to Eurocopter back in December 2009 for 111 million USD, with option for 17 more EC-225 helicopter. Expect delivery of 3 EC-225 by October 2011.

On August 31, 2010, it was announced for next year's defense budget, ROCAF's "Medium Transport aircraft" plan to replace 12 B-1900 VIP/transport training aircraft, believe to be 6-8+ Lockheed C-27J, has been put on hold and might be axed, due to lack of budget. But will allocates 20+ million US dollars over next 4 years for quick runway repair. Other items mentioned including increases runways from 3 to 6 at Easter Taiwan's 3 airbases, moving 2 I-HAWK batteries to Eastern Taiwan to protect those airbases, which will double to 4 batteries, and others.ROCN plan to lease 1 or 2 more Newport LSTs from US, but the 900 ton stealth corvette plan has been put on hold, due to lack of budget. ROCA plan for next generation MBT has been put on hold, due to lack of budget.

On September 29, 2010, the U.S. Congress passed resolution, authorizing U.S. government for sales of 1 more Osprey class mine hunter to Taiwan.

Reforms and development

Civilian control of the military

The modern day ROC military is styled after western military systems, mostly the US military. Internally, it has a very strong political warfare branch/department that tightly controls and monitors each level of the ROC military, and reports directly to the General Headquarters of the ROC military, and if necessary, directly to the President of the ROC. This is a carry over from the pre-1949 era, when the KMT and its army were penetrated by Communist agents repeatedly, leading to front line units defecting to Communist China. To strengthen his control over the military, and prevent defections after the retreat to Taiwan in 1949, CKS and CCK retained tight control over military, installing political officers and commissioners down to the company level, in order to ensure political correctness in the military and loyalty toward ROC leadership. This gave the political officers/commissioners a great deal of power, allowing them to overrule the unit commander and take over the unit. Only in recent years has the political warfare department reduced its power within the ROC military, due to cutbacks.

Two defense reform laws implemented in 2002 granted the civilian defence minister control over the entire military and expanded legislative oversight authority for the first time in history. But still as in the past, Chief of Staff of General HQ still the most powerful military position in ROC military with broader power than Defense Minister, even though he suppose to be an adviser to the Defense Minister and President under the laws. In the past the ROC military was closely linked with and controlled by the Kuomintang (Nationalist Party). Following the democratization of the 1990s the military has moved to a politically neutral position, though the senior officer ranks remain dominated by KMT members.

Doctrine and exercises

The primary goal of the ROC Armed Forces is to provide a credible deterrent against hostile action by establishing effective counterstrike and defense capabilities. Should hostilities occur, current ROC military doctrine centers upon the principle of "offshore engagement" where the primary goal of the armed forces in any conflict with the PRC would be to keep as much of the fighting away from Taiwan proper for as long as possible to minimize damage to infrastructure and civilian casualties. The military has also begun to take the threat of a sudden "decapitation attack" by the PRC seriously. Consequently, these developments have seen a growing emphasis on the role of the Navy and Air Force (where the Army had traditionally dominated); as well as the development of rapid reaction forces and quick mobilization of local reserve forces.

ROCAF AIDC F-CK Indigenous Defence Fighter

Annually, the ROC Military conducts full exercises called "Han Kuang" which may sometimes include all branches of the military to participate in one or two specific exercises, they show the Taiwanese media the various weapons they have acquired and give special performances from the army, navy and air force. "Han Kuang" exercises are held throughout Taiwan mainly at the main expected invasion areas. In 2007 there was an army exercise simulating a counterattack against PLA forces who have captured Taichung Port. An air force exercise simulating that air bases throughout Taiwan have been destroyed and are forced to use a major highway as an airstrip. ROCN (navy) exercise where an invasion force is heading toward Taiwan, destroyers, frigates and attack boats are called to fire missiles and attack dummy targets.

Foreign cooperation

Japan

Singapore

Starting in 1975, Singapore has sent units from its military to train in Taiwan due to the lack of space in the city-state under the Starlight training program (星光計畫). Singaporean forces training in Taiwan numbered roughly 3000 as of 2005. As of 2008, Singapore is the only foreign country to maintain permanent military bases on Taiwan.

Singapore being an island surrounded by larger countries found similarity with Taiwan; this might have contributed to its suitability as a training ground. However this became a point of conflict between Singapore and Beijing. Beijing demanded the withdrawal of troops and offered to provide another training ground on Hainan Island. Singapore refused the offer, rather stated it would withdraw its forces and not take part in any confrontation.

United States

Collaboration between the ROC and US militaries began during World War II when both nations were members of the Allied forces, and continued through the Chinese Civil War when ROC forces were supplied primarily by the US until the final evacuation of ROC forces to Taiwan in 1949. Initially the U.S. expected the ROC government to fall and withdrew support until the outbreak of the Korean War when the U.S. 7th Fleet was ordered to the Taiwan Straits both to protect Taiwan from a PRC attack, and to stop ROC actions against the PRC. A formal US-ROC security pact was signed in 1954 establishing a formal alliance that lasted until US recognition of the PRC in 1979. During this period US military advisors were deployed to the ROC and joint exercises were common. The United States Taiwan Defense Command was established in the Philippines for reinforcement of the Taiwan airspace. The US and ROC also collaborated on human and electronic intelligence operations directed against the PRC. ROC units also participated in the Korean War and the Vietnam War in noncombat capacities, primarily at the insistence of the United States which was concerned that high profile roles for ROC forces in these conflicts would lead to full scale PRC intervention.

High-level cooperation ended with the US recognition of the PRC in 1979, when all remaining US forces in Taiwan were withdrawn. The US continued to supply the ROC with arms sales per the Taiwan Relations Act, albeit in a diminished role. While ROCAF pilots continued to train at Luke AFB in Arizona, cooperation is still limited primarily to civilian contractors.

In recent years, the ROC military has again begun higher level cooperation with the U.S. Military after over two decades of relative isolation. Senior officers from the U.S. Pacific Command observed the annual Han Kuang military exercises in 2005. The US also upgraded its military liaison position in Taipei from a position held by retired officers hired on a contractual basis to one held by an active duty officer the same year. The US remains committed to protecting Taiwan from PRC attack, though not if the ROC were to declare formal independence first - Washington has stated it will not back such a declaration with military support.

Others

The political warfare department of ROC military had trained officers from other pro US/Western/Taiwan nations in Central and Southern America, Africa, Middle East, and South East Asia, from 1950s to 1980s. Most of these officers later held military powers in their respective country or became dictators. Good examples would be Col. Muammar Abu Minyar al-QADHAFI of Libya, and Manuel Noriega of Panama.

Military parades

The Republic of China held their first military parade on 10 October 2007 for National Day celebrations since 1991. Previously parades weren't held as the government tried to ease the tension between ROC and the PRC and to try and promote peace, however ever since the military balance started to favour Beijing, the ROC government has been under pressure to deter Communist China. The military parade was designed to act as a deterrent to Beijing.

The parade unveiled the ROC's new indigenous Hsiung Feng III Supersonic Anti-Ship missiles, Sky Bow III Surface to Air missiles and a few of the ROC's very own Chung Shyang II UAVs. However the expected unveiling of the Hsiung Feng IIE Land Attack Cruise Missile which could reach Shanghai was not unveiled as the defence minister stated that it was still under development. Military aircraft including the US made F-16 A/Bs & F-5s, French produced Mirage 2000-5s and domestically made IDFs flew past the parade area in formation. US made AH-1W Super Cobras, CH-47SD Chinooks, UH-1H Huey & S-70C(M)1/2 Thunderhawk helicopters and E-2C Hawkeye 2000, S-2T Tracker & C-130H Hercules aircraft also flew past. Cadets then filled the main area, and performed various march formation and tricks with their rifles. Military police then drove out in style with their Harley-Davidson bikes numbering in total of around 50. The new CM-32 APCs, AAVP7 Amphibious Assault Vehicles, HUMVEEs fitted with BGM-71 TOW 2nd generation anti-tank missiles and FGM-148 Javelin anti-tank missiles, Avengers anti-air vehicles, M48 Chaparral anti-air vehicles fitted with Sidewinder missiles and other various vehicles were driven out in order. Sky Bow I, Sky Bow II & Sky Bow III missiles, PATRIOT missiles and Hsiung Feng II & Hsiung Feng III anti-ship missiles with their launchers were driven out and showcased in front of the large crowd. Meanwhile, Taiwanese marines, army special forces and counter terrorist units were driven out in vehicles with various new weaponry including the home made T-91 rifle, customised M4A1s and M16s with attachments and the newly purchased MP5s.[1]

Military ranks

Main article: Republic of China Armed Forces rank insignia

The ROC military's rank structure is patterned after that of the U.S. Armed Forces. Note that the titles of each rank are the same in Chinese for all four military branches. The corresponding titles in English for each service are also provided.

ROC Officer Ranks

Chinese title	Army / Marines / MP	Navy	Air Force
一級/二級上將	General	Admiral	General
中將	Lieutenant General	Vice Admiral	Lieutenant General
少將	Major General	Rear Admiral	Major General
上校	Colonel	Captain	Colonel
中校	Lieutenant Colonel	Commander	Lieutenant Colonel
少校	Major	Lieutenant Commander	Major
上尉	Captain	Lieutenant	Captain
中尉	1st Lieutenant	Lieutenant Junior Grade	1st Lieutenant
少尉	2nd Lieutenant	Ensign	2nd Lieutenant

ROC Enlisted Ranks

Chinese title	Army / Marines / MP	Navy	Air Force
一等士官長	Sergeant Major	Master Chief Petty Officer	Chief Master Sergeant
二等士官長	Master Sergeant	Senior Chief Petty Officer	Senior Master Sergeant
三等士官長	Sergeant First Class	Chief Petty Officer	Master Sergeant
上士	Staff Sergeant	Petty Officer 1st Class	Technical Sergeant
中士	Sergeant	Petty Officer 2nd Class	Staff Sergeant
下士	Corporal	Petty Officer 3rd Class	Senior Airman
上等兵	Private First Class	Seaman First Class	Airman First Class
一等兵	Private	Seaman	Airman
二等兵	Private Basic	Seaman Apprentice	Airman Basic

Major deployments, battles and incidents

1912–1949

ROC soldiers marching to the front lines in 1939

- Northern Expedition: 1926–1928
- Central Plains War: May 1930 – November 4, 1930
- First Communist Insurrection/Purge: 1927–1937
  - Nanchang Uprising: 1927
  - Autumn Harvest Uprising: 1927
  - Xi'an Incident: December 12, 1936
- Second Sino-Japanese War/World War II: 1937–1945
  - Marco Polo Bridge Incident: July 7, 1937
  - Battle of Shanghai: August 13 - November 9, 1937
  - Battle of Nanjing: October-December, 1937
  - Battle of Taierzhuang: March 24 - April 7, 1938
  - First Battle of Changsha: September 17 – October 6, 1939
  - Second Battle of Changsha: September 6 – October 8, 1941
  - Third Battle of Changsha: December 24, 1941 – January 15, 1942
  - Defense of Sichuan: 1942–1943
  - Battle of Hengyang-Changsha: June 1944 – April 1945
- Chinese Civil War: 1946–1950
  - New Fourth Army Incident: 1940
- 228 Incident: February 28 - March 1947

1949–present

- Battle of Kuningtou: October 25–28, 1949
- Battle of Denbu Island: November 3 – 5, 1949
- First Battle of Dadan Island: July 26, 1950
- Battle of Nanri island: April 11 – 15, 1952
- Dongshan Island Campaign: July 15, 1953
- First Taiwan Strait Crisis: August 1954 – May 1955
  - Battle of Yijiangshan: January 18, 1955
  - Tachen Evacuation: February 7–11, 1955
- Second Taiwan Strait Crisis: August 23 – early October 1958
  - Second Battle of Dadan island: August 26, 1958
- Vietnam War: 1960s, Under CIA direction, deployment of small groups of ROC troops disguised as locals, transportation, and technical assistance, under guise of Taiwan/ROC state owned China Air Lines, with 34th "Black Bat" Squadron personnel and ROCAF aircraft fleet of C-46, C-47, C-54, C-123B/K and P2V-7U/RB-69A under Project South Star I, II, and III, aka to USAF as Det 1 of USAF 75th Troop Carrier Squadron, aka First Flight Detachment(FED) of CIA's better known Studies and Observations Group(SOG), that besides fulfilled transportation needs, also provided covert ESM missions, resupply airdrops and agent insertions in Laos and North Vietnam. Also sent LST fleet to the region during the last days of Vietnam War. Not widely publicized to avoid PRC involvement.
- Battle of Dong-Yin: May 1, 1965
- Battle of Wuchow: November 13–14, 1965
- Yemen Civil War: 1979 to 1985: 80+ F-5E pilots plus ground crew sent to North Yemen to boost its air defense, under US support/direction. At least one squadron strength was kept through out the period, flying North Yemen's F-5E fleet.
- Third Taiwan Strait Crisis: July 21, 1995 – March 23, 1996
- Southeast Asian tsunami relief: January 2005

ROCN honor guard at the Martyr's Shrine in Taipei.

Nuclear weapons program

The development of nuclear weapons by the ROC has been a contentious issue, as it has been cited by the PRC as a reason to attack Taiwan. The U.S., hoping to avoid escalating tensions in the Taiwan Strait, has continually opposed arming the ROC with nuclear weapons. Accordingly, the ROC adheres to the principles of the nuclear Non-Proliferation Treaty and has stated that it does not intend to produce nuclear weapons. Past nuclear research by the ROC makes it a 'threshold' nuclear state.

In 1967, a nuclear weapons program began under the auspices of the Institute of Nuclear Energy Research (INER) at the Chungshan Institute of Science and Technology. The ROC was able to acquire nuclear technology from abroad (including a research reactor from Canada and low-grade plutonium from the United States) allegedly for a civilian energy system, but in actuality to develop fuel for nuclear weapons.

After the International Atomic Energy Agency found evidence of the ROC's efforts to produce weapons-grade plutonium, Taipei agreed in September 1976 under U.S. pressure to dismantle its nuclear weapons program. Though the nuclear reactor was soon shut down and the plutonium mostly returned to the U.S., work continued secretly.

A secret program was revealed when Colonel Chang Hsien-yi, deputy director of nuclear research at INER who was secretly working for the CIA defected to the U.S. in December 1987 and produced a cache of incriminating documents. General Hau Pei-tsun claimed that scientists in Taiwan had already produced a controlled nuclear reaction. Under pressure from the U.S., the program was halted.

During the 1995-1996 Taiwan Strait crisis, then ROC President Lee Teng-hui proposed to reactivate the program, but was forced to back down a few days later after drawing intense criticism.

See also

	**This article contains Chinese text.** Without proper rendering support, you may see question marks, boxes, or other symbols instead of Chinese characters.

- Whampoa Military Academy
- Chungshan Institute of Science and Technology
- Republic of China Armed Forces Museum

External links

- ROC Ministry of National Defense Official Website (Chinese) [2] (English) [3]
- The Armed Forces Museum of ROC [4]

Whampoa Military Academy

Whampoa Military Academy

Geographical coordinates: 23°5′22.5″N 113°25′13″E

The **Nationalist Party of China Army Officer Academy** (traditional Chinese: 中國國民黨陸軍軍官學校; simplified Chinese: 中国国民党陆军军官学校; pinyin: *Zhōngguó Guómíndǎng Lùjūn Jūnguān Xuéxiào*), commonly known as the **Whampoa Military Academy** (traditional Chinese: 黃埔軍校; simplified Chinese: 黄埔军校; pinyin: *Huángpǔ Jūnxiào*), was a military academy in the Republic of China (ROC) that produced many prestigious commanders who fought in many of China's conflicts in the 20th century, notably the Northern Expedition, the Second Sino-Japanese War and the Chinese Civil War.

The Whampoa Military Academy emblem includes its motto, which was first proclaimed by Sun Yat-sen at the Whampoa Academy's opening in 1924. It translates into "**Fraternity, Dexterity, Sincerity**."

The military academy was officially opened on June 16, 1924 under the Kuomintang (KMT), but the first lessons began on May 1, 1924. The inauguration was on Changzhou Island offshore from the Whampoa dock in Guangzhou, thus earning its common name. During the inaugural ceremonies, Sun Yat-sen delivered a speech that was later to become the lyrics of the national anthem of the Republic of China.

Establishment

After the death of Yuan Shikai, China fragmented into numerous fiefdoms ruled by warlords. Sun Yat-sen attempted in 1917 and 1920 to set up a base in his native Guangdong to launch a northern campaign to unite China under his Three Principles of the People. However, his government remained militarily weaker than local warlords armies. Calls by Sun for arms and money were ignored by the western powers.

National Revolution Army flag

In 1921 the representative of Comintern, Henk Sneevliet (using the name Maring), met with Sun in Guangxi. He proposed to set up a military academy and train the revolutionary army, which confirmed Sun's ideas and he eventually accepted. The Chinese Communist Party sent Li Dazhao and Lin Boqu (林伯渠) to discuss with Sun and his party on how to set up this academy.

Sun Yat-sen [middle behind the table] and Chiang Kai-shek [on stage in uniform] at the founding of the Whampoa Military Academy in 1924.

In 1924, in the 1st National Congress of Kuomintang, the policy of alliance with the Soviet Union and CCP was passed as guidance for KMT. As a result, the final decision of establishment of a military academy was made and preparatory committee was set up accordingly. The money necessary for the construction and support of the Academy in 1924-1925 was provided by the Soviets.

Organization, Training and Students

Commandant Chiang Kai-shek inspecting cadets of the Whampoa Military Academy.

In the beginning, the Academy had only one department which provided soldiers with basic training. While the main Academy goal was preparation of infantry units, it also provided special classes for artillery, engineering, communication, logistical and machine gun units. A special department for preparation of political agitators was established later.

The academy concentrated the revolutionary military talents at the time. Sun took the job of Premier of this academy in person although it was just an honorary title. Sun's favorite and rising star Chiang Kai-shek was appointed the first commandant of the academy. Liao Zhongkai (廖仲愷), the famous leftist of Kuomintang and Sun's treasury secretary, was appointed as representative of KMT to the academy. Zhou Enlai, Hu Han-min and Wang Ching-wei were among the instructors in the political department. He Yingqin and Ye Jianying were once military instructors.

The serious lack of expert teachers was the biggest problem for the Academy. That is why lectures delivered by Soviet officers were extremely popular among students. A.S. Bubnov, G.I. Gilev, M.I. Dratvin, S.N. Naumov prepared lectures which explained the development of military thought throughout human history and the division between western and Soviet schools of military thought.

Ex-officers of the Russian White Army, who switched to the Soviet side after 1917, taught different military subjects in the Academy using their broad experience gained during the Russian Civil War. Among them were I. Vasilevich (Janovsky), N. Korneev, M. Nefedov, F. Kotov (Katyushin), P. Lunev, V. Akimov. Galina Kolchugina (wife of Vasily Blyukher who was Commander-in-Chief of all Soviet volunteer forces sent to China) read a course of lectures on political agitation.

Vasily Blyukher, Commander of Soviet volunteer forces

The first two groups of students prepared by the Academy became the core for the formation of the first two National Revolutionary Army regiments (V.A. Stepanov was an advisor provided by the Soviet Union to help in this matter). The first two prepared groups of students included 500 officers, the third one had 800 officers and the fourth had 2000.

Legendary graduates included Communist commanders Lin Biao, Xu Xiangqian, Zuo Quan (左權), Chen Geng (陳賡), and Nationalist commanders Chen Cheng, Du Yuming, Xue Yue, and Hu Zongnan. These young students first showed their training and courage in the war against local warlord and dissident of Sun, Chen Jiongming (陳炯明), and later the unification of Guangdong province. Then they made greater contributions in the Northern Expedition.

The muslim Ma clique General Ma Zhongying, who commanded the 36th Division (National Revolutionary Army), attended the Whampoa military academy in Nanjing in 1929.

Influence

The Whampoa Military Academy plays an important role in Chinese history. Although it is primarily a military academy aiming to train military elites like the United States Military Academy, it has exhibited a broad influence on Chinese history. It not only supplied many military commanders for both the KMT and CCP, but also its graduates have much more influence on both parties' policies and governance.

Modern picture of the Whampoa Military Academy.

Especially for Chiang and KMT, the Whampoa Clique was pivotal for his governance. It competed with other cliques of KMT such as the New Guangxi Clique led by Li Zongren and Bai Chongxi, CC Clique led by Chen Lifu and Chen Guofu, Politics Research Group led by Yang Yongtai (楊永泰) and Zhang Qun (張群). At the same time, when the CCP built its first Red Army after the Nanchang Uprising in 1927 most of its commanders were from Whampoa, and in the following two decades, the CCP trained its army in the Whampoa way.

The motto of the academy "Camaraderie" (親愛精誠, literally 'Fraternity, Dexterity, Sincerity') was proclaimed by Sun Yat-sen at the opening ceremonies. The irony is that during the Chinese Civil War both the commanders from KMT and CCP were trained and educated in Whampoa. They fought for different beliefs and ideals although they used to live and study together like brothers in arms.

The academy also had significant influence over the 20th century history of other Asian countries. The fourth term of the Academy saw students not only from all parts of China, but also from different parts of Asia enroll. For example, there were 30 Koreans among them. Some of them were brought up in China, others were active participants during the national liberation movement of Korea in 1917-1926 and emigrated to China later only to take up arms for struggle for freedom of their country after their education was over.

A large number of students were originally from Vietnam. This group was led by an exiled to-be leader of the Communist Party of Vietnam and Vietnamese struggle for independence Ho Chi Minh.

Relocations

The original Whampoa Military Academy existed from 1924 to 1926, over 6 terms it enrolled more than 7000. However, Chiang Kai-shek purged the Chinese Communist Party during the Northern Expedition the academy was moved to the newly established capital in Nanjing after the defeat of the warlords in 1928. The academy moved again to Chengdu during the Japanese invasion.

The gate of Whampoa Military Academy

Republic of China Military Academy

Main article: Republic of China Military Academy

In 1950, after the Communist victory on mainland China and the establishment of the People's Republic of China, the academy was re-established in Fongshan, Kaohsiung County, Taiwan as the Chinese Military Academy (陸軍官校) and changed name in 2004 to the Military University. (軍官大學) The site of the original academy in Guangzhou is now a museum.

See also

This article contains Chinese text. Without proper rendering support, you may see question marks, boxes, or other symbols instead of Chinese characters.

- National Revolutionary Army
- Chiang Kai-shek
- Kuomintang
- Warlord era
- Sino-German cooperation
- History of the Republic of China
- Military of the Republic of China

External links

- The Chinese Military Academy Official Website [1]
- Audio file: RTHK broadcast in Cantonese [2]
- Article: "China to Turn Site of KMT Military Academy into Tourist Spot" [3] on the *People's Daily* website

National Revolutionary Army

National Revolutionary Army

National Revolutionary Army (NRA) 國民革命軍	
Flag of the National Revolutionary Army	
Active	1925 – 1947
Country	Republic of China
Allegiance	Kuomintang (KMT) Republic of China (ROC)
Type	Army
Engagements	Northern Expedition Long March Second Sino-Japanese War Chinese Civil War
Commanders	
Notable commanders	Chiang Kai-shek Zhang Xueliang Yen Hsi-shan Feng Yuxiang Sun Li-jen He Yingqin Hu Kexian and many others

The **National Revolutionary Army** (**NRA**) (simplified Chinese: 国民革命军; traditional Chinese: 國民革命軍; pinyin: *Guómín Gémìng Jūn*, sometimes shortened to 國軍 or **National Army**) was the Military Arm of the Kuomintang (KMT) from 1925 until 1947, as well as the national army of the

Republic of China during the KMT's period of party rule beginning in 1928.

Originally organized with Soviet aid as a means for the KMT to unify China against warlordism, the National Revolutionary Army fought major engagements in the Northern Expedition against the Chinese Beiyang Army warlords, in the Second Sino-Japanese War against the Imperial Japanese Army, and in the Chinese Civil War against the People's Liberation Army.

During the Second Sino-Japanese War, the armed forces of the Communist Party of China were nominally incorporated into the National Revolutionary Army (while retaining separate commands), but broke away to form the People's Liberation Army shortly after the end of the war. With the promulgation of the Constitution of the Republic of China in 1947 and the formal end of the KMT party-state, the National Revolutionary Army was renamed the Military of the Republic of China (中華民國國軍), with the bulk of its forces forming the Republic of China Army, which retreated to Taiwan in 1949.

History

The NRA was founded by the Kuomintang in 1925 as the military force destined to unite China in the Northern Expedition. Organized with the help of the Comintern and guided under the doctrine of the Three Principles of the People, the distinction among party, state, and army was often blurred. A large number of the Army's officers passed through the Whampoa Military Academy, and the first commandant, Chiang Kai-shek, became commander-in-chief of the Army in 1925 before launching the successful Northern Expedition. Aside from Chiang Kai-shek himself, other prominent commanders in the National Revolutionary Army included Du Yuming and Chen Cheng.

The NRA during WWII

A Chinese Nationalist soldier, age 10, member of a Chinese division from the X Force, boarding planes in Burma bound for China, May 1944.

Organization

The National Revolutionary Army soldiers marched into the British concessions in Hankou during the Northern Expedition.

The NRA throughout its lifespan recruited approximately 4,300,000 regulars, in 370 Standard Divisions (正式師), 46 New Divisions (新編師), 12 Cavalry Divisions (騎兵師), eight New Cavalry Divisions (新編騎兵師), 66 Temporary Divisions (暫編師), and 13 Reserve Divisions (預備師), for a grand total of 515 divisions. However, many divisions were formed from two or more other divisions, and were not active at the same time.

Also, New Divisions were created to replace Standard Divisions lost early in the war and were issued the old division's number. Therefore the number of divisions in active service at any given time is much smaller than this. The average NRA division had 5,000–6,000 troops; an average army had 10,000–15,000 troops, the equivalent of a Japanese division. The German-trained divisions were not even on par in terms of manpower with a German or Japanese division, having only 10,000 troops.

The NRA only had small number of armoured vehicles and mechanised troops. At the beginning of the war in 1937 the armour were organized in three Armoured Battalions, equipped with tanks and armoured cars from various countries. After these battalions were mostly destroyed in the Battle of Shanghai and Battle of Nanjing new tanks, armoured cars and trucks from the Soviet Union and Italy made it possible to create the only mechanized division in the army, the 200th Division. This Division eventually ceased to be a mechanized unit after the June 1938 reorganization of Divisions. The armoured and artillery Regiments were placed under direct command of 5th Corps and the 200th Division became a motorized Infantry Division within the same Corps. This Corps fought battles in Guangxi in 1939–1940 and in Burma in 1942 reducing the armored units due to losses and mechanical breakdown of the vehicles.

On paper China had 3.8 million men under arms in 1941. They were organized into 246 "front-line" divisions, with another 70 divisions assigned to rear areas. Perhaps as many as forty Chinese divisions had been equipped with European-manufactured weapons and trained by foreign, particularly German and Soviet, advisers. The rest of the units were under strength and generally untrained. Overall, the Nationalist Army impressed most Western military observers as more reminiscent of a nineteenth- than a twentieth-century army.

A group of NRA soldiers from Sun Li-jen's New First Army marching off while a P-40 Warhawk flies overhead. Notice the soldiers are wearing American M1 Helmets.

Late in the Burma Campaign the NRA Army there had an armoured battalion equipped with Sherman tanks.

Despite the poor views given by European observers on the European trained Divisions, the Muslim Divisions of the National Revolutionary Army, trained in China, not by westerners, and led by the Ma Clique Muslim Generals, frightened the European observers with their appearance and fighting skills in battle. Europeans like Sven Hedin and Georg Vasel were in awe of the appearance Chinese Muslim NRA divisions and their ferocious combat abilities. They were trained in harsh, brutal conditions. The 36th Division (National Revolutionary Army), trained entirely in China, without any European help, was composed of Chinese muslims, fought against and severely mauled an invading Soviet Russian army during the Soviet Invasion of Xinjiang. The division was inferior in technology and manpower, but slammed the superior Russian force.

The Muslim divisions of the army controlled by Muslim General Ma Honkui were reported by western observers to be tough and disciplined. Despite having diabetes, Ma Hongkui personally drilled with his troops, and engaged in sword fencing during training.

The unit organisation of the NRA is as follows: (Note that a unit is not necessarily subordinate to one immediately above it; several army regiments can be found under an army group, for example.)

National Military Council

- Military Region ×12 (軍區)
    - Army Corps ×4(兵團)
        - Army Group ×40 (集團軍 *Group Army*)
            - Route Army (路軍)
            - Army ×30 (軍)
                - Corps ×133 (軍團 *Army Group*)
                    - Division (師)
                        - Brigade (旅)
                            - Regiment (團)
                                - Battalion (營)
                                    - Company (連)
                                        - Platoon (排)
                                            - Squad (班)

Commander-in-chief

- Chiang Kai-shek 1925–1947

Equipment

Main articles: Development of Chinese armoured forces (1927-1945) and Development of Chinese Nationalist air force (1937–1945)

Major Chinese Arsenals:

Browning HP 9mm pistol manufactured by John Inglis in Canada during 1944–1945 for forces in Burma. The Chinese inscription says "Property of the Republic of China".

Province	Arsenal Name
Kwangtung	Guangdong Arsenal
Honan	Kung Hsien Arsenal
Manchuria	Mukden Arsenal
Hupei	Hangyang Arsenal
Shansi	Taiyuan Arsenal
Szechwan	Chengtu Arsenal

Chinese weapons were mainly produced for the National Revolutionary Army in the Hanyang, Guangdong and Taiyuan Arsenals.

For regular Chinese divisions their standard rifles were the Hanyang 88 (copy of Gewehr 88) and Chiang Kai-Shek rifle (copy of Mauser Standard Model). However, for most of the German-trained divisions, the standard firearms were German-made 7.92 mm Gewehr 98 and Karabiner 98k. The standard light machine gun was a local copy of the Czech 7.92 mm Brno ZB26. There were also Belgian and French light machine guns. Surprisingly, the NRA did not purchase any Maschinengewehr 34s from Germany, but did produce their own copies of them. On average in these divisions, there was one light machine gun set for each platoon. Heavy machine guns were mainly locally-made Type 24 water-cooled Maxim guns, which is the Chinese copy of the German MG08. On average every battalion would get one heavy machine gun (about a third to half of what actual German divisions got during World War II). The standard sidearm was the 7.63 mm Mauser C96 semi-automatic pistol, or full-automatic Mauser M1932/M712 machine pistol. These full-automatic versions were used as substitutes for submachine guns (such as the MP18) and rifles that were in short supply within the Chinese army prior to the end of World War II. During the Second Sino-Japanese War, the NRA also extensively used captured Japanese weapons and equipment as their own were slightly in short supply. Some élite units also used Lend-Lease US equipment as the war progressed.

Some divisions were equipped with 37 mm PaK 35/36 anti-tank guns, and/or mortars from Oerlikon, Madsen, and Solothurn. Each infantry division had 6 French Brandt 81 mm mortars and 6 Solothurn 20 mm autocannons. Some independent brigades and artillery regiments were equipped with Bofors 72 mm L/14, or Krupp 72 mm L/29 mountain guns and there were 24 Rheinmetall 150 mm L/32 sFH 18 howitzers (bought in 1934) and 24 Krupp 150 mm L/30 sFH 18 howitzers (bought in 1936).

Infantry uniforms were basically redesigned Zhongshan suits. Puttees were standard for soldiers and officers alike since the primary mode of movement for NRA troops was by foot. The helmets were the most distinguishing characteristic of these divisions. From the moment German M35 helmets (standard issue for the Wehrmacht until late in the European theatre) rolled off the production lines in 1935, and until 1936, the NRA imported 315,000 of these helmets, each with the Blue Sky with a White Sun emblem of the ROC on the sides. Other helmets include the Adrian helmet, Brodie helmet and later M1 helmet. Other equipment included cloth shoes for soldiers, leather shoes for officers and leather boots for high-ranking officers. Every soldier was issued ammunition, ammunition pouch or harness, a water flask, combat knives, food bag, and a gas mask.

Spears and swords in addition to rifles were used by the Muslim Ma Clique sections of the National Revolutionary Army. The muslims had an assortment of rifles, german, british, russian, and others.

Gallery

The cavalry of the National Revolutionary Army.

The cavalry of the National Revolutionary Army charging with Dadaos. One of them has what appears to be a pistol.

National Revolutionary Army soldiers manning a Czech ZB vz. 26 Light Machine Gun. Note the Blue-Sky White Sun insignia on the Brodie helmets.

National Revolutionary army soldiers wearing the M35 Stahlhelm in a parade.

German-trained Nationalist Soldiers Marching with Gewehr 98 rifles.

Foreign suppliers

- Belgium
- Canada
- Czechoslovakia
- Denmark
- France
- Germany
- Italy
- Soviet Union
- United Kingdom
- United States

See also

- German-trained divisions of the National Revolutionary Army
- Whampoa Military Academy
- Warlord era
- Chiang Kai-shek
- Sino-German cooperation
- Military of the Republic of China
- History of the Republic of China
- Military of the People's Republic of China
- Chinese Army in India
- Chinese Expeditionary Force (in Burma)
- Republic of China Navy

External links

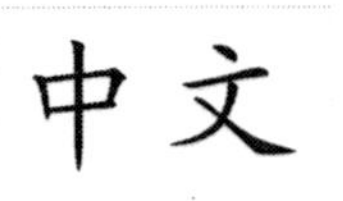	**This article contains Chinese text.** Without proper rendering support, you may see question marks, boxes, or other symbols instead of Chinese characters.

- ROC Ministry of National Defense Official Website [3]
- The Armed Forces Museum of ROC [4]
- Information and pictures of Nationalist Revolutionary Army weapons and equipment [1]
- rare pictures of NRA heavy armory [2]
- more pictures of NRA [3]

Republic of China Military Academy

Republic of China Military Academy

The **Republic of China Military Academy** (Chinese: 中華民國陸軍軍官學校, pinyin: Zhōnghúa Mīngúo Lùjūn Jūnguān Xúexiào, literally "Republic of China Army Officer School; or abbreviated Chinese: 陸軍官校, pinyin: Lùjūn Guānxiào, literally "Army Officer School"), also known as the **Chinese Military Academy** (CMA), is the military academy of the Republic of China and is located in Fengshan, Kaohsiung County, Taiwan.

The CMA emblem includes its motto, which was first proclaimed by Sun Yat-sen at the Whampoa Academy's opening in 1924. It translates into "Fraternity, Devotion, Sincerity."

Heritage & purpose

Established in 1950 after the loss of mainland China by the Kuomintang in the Chinese Civil War the academy traces its roots to the Whampoa Military Academy and observes many of its traditions. Modelled after the United States Military Academy, its four-year program trains officers for the Army of the Republic of China.

See also

- Republic of China Naval Academy
- Republic of China Air Force Academy

External links

- Official site [1]

Republic of China and weapons of mass destruction

Republic of China and weapons of mass destruction

Weapons of mass destruction	
By type	
Biological, Chemical, Nuclear, Radiological	
By country	
Albania	Libya
Algeria	Netherlands
Argentina	North Korea
Australia	Pakistan
Brazil	Poland
Bulgaria	Romania
Burma	Russia
Canada	Saudi Arabia
PR	South Africa
China	Sweden
France	Syria
Germany	Taiwan (ROC)
India	Ukraine
Iran	United
Iraq	Kingdom
Israel	United States
Japan	
Proliferation	

Biological, Chemical, Nuclear, Missiles
Treaties
List of treaties
Book · Category

The **Republic of China (ROC)**, also known as **Taiwan**, denies having any **weapons of mass destruction**. There is currently no evidence of Taiwan possessing any chemical or nuclear weapons.

Nuclear weapons

Research program

In 1967, a nuclear weapons program began under the auspices of the Institute of Nuclear Energy Research (INER) at the Chungshan Institute of Science and Technology. Taiwan was able to acquire nuclear technology from abroad (including a research reactor from Canada and low-grade plutonium from the United States) allegedly for a civilian energy system, but in actuality to develop fuel for nuclear weapons.

During the 1970s, Taiwan had an active program to produce plutonium using heavy water reactors. However, after the International Atomic Energy Agency found evidence of Taiwan's efforts to produce weapons-grade plutonium, Taipei agreed in September 1976 under U.S. pressure to dismantle its nuclear weapons program. U.S. Intelligence believed Taiwan also had designed devices suitable for nuclear testing.

A secret program was revealed when Colonel Chang Hsien-yi, deputy director of nuclear research at INER who was secretly working for the CIA defected to the U.S. in December 1987 and produced a cache of incriminating documents. General Hau Pei-tsun claimed that scientists in Taiwan had already produced a controlled nuclear reaction. Under pressure from the U.S., the program was halted.

During the 1995-1996 Taiwan Strait crisis, then Taiwan President Lee Teng-hui proposed to reactivate the program, but was forced to back down a few days later after drawing intense criticism.

Current status

There is no evidence that the ROC possesses any nuclear weapons or any current programs to produce them, although it does have the general technological ability to develop the ability to enrich uranium or process plutonium. All of Taiwan's nuclear power plants currently use imported enriched uranium and are subject to International Atomic Energy Agency inspection.

The People's Republic of China has announced that any Taiwanese possession of nuclear weapons is grounds for an immediate attack. Attempts by ROC officials to form a dialogue with the PRC on the subject of WMDs have been rebuffed.

Chemical weapons

Taiwan may be in possession of small quantities of sarin. However, the Taiwan government has stated that any such materials are only for defensive research purposes and that it does not have any intention of producing offensive chemical weapons.

Ratification of international treaties

The Republic of China ratified the Geneva Protocol on August 7, 1929 and the Nuclear Non-Proliferation Treaty (NPT) in 1970. Following UN General Assembly Resolution 2758 (1971) the United Nations does not recognize the Republic of China as a legitimate political entity, and as such does not recognize any right that the ROC has to join international multilateral treaties. Because of its controversial political status, the ROC has not been allowed to join either the Biological Weapons Convention nor the Chemical Weapons Convention, but it has stated that it will abide by both treaties nevertheless. In addition, it has stated that it will continue to abide by the NPT, notwithstanding controversy over its political status.

See also

- National Revolutionary Army
- Whampoa Military Academy
- Chiang Kai-shek
- History of the Republic of China
- Military of the Republic of China
- Kuomintang
- List of states with nuclear weapons
- Timeline of the Republic of China's nuclear program

External links

- Deployments by country, 1951-1977 [1] The Bulletin of the Atomic Scientists [2], Nov/Dec 1999
- United States Secretly Deployed Nuclear Bombs In 27 Countries and Territories During Cold War [3]

Wucih Mountain Military Cemetery

Wuchih Mountain Military Cemetery

Wuzhi Mountain Military Cemetery	
Traditional Chinese	五指山國軍示範公墓
Simplified Chinese	五指山国军示范公墓
Transliterations	
Mandarin	
- Hanyu Pinyin	Wǔzhǐ Shān Guójūn Shìfàn Gōngmù

The cemetery has a wide open view ranging from the Taipei 101 over at Taipei's Xinyi District to the Keelung Harbor.

The cemetery, which has 9,417 grave plots, is nearly full; further deceased military officials will need to be cremated and their ashes stored in the columbarium.

Notable interments

- Chiang Wei-kuo, adopted son of Chiang Kai-shek
- He Yingqin, a senior KMT general
- Yen Chia-kan, former president of the ROC

See also

- Cihu Presidential Burial Place
- Touliao Mausoleum

Republic of China Military Police

Republic of China Military Police

Republic of China Military Police	
Active	1913 - Present
Country	Republic of China
Branch	Military Police
Size	16,000 (2004 est.)
Part of	Republic of China Armed Forces
Garrison/HQ	Taipei City, Republic of China
Anniversaries	December 12th
Engagements	Northern Expedition Xi'an Incident Second Sino-Japanese War Chinese Civil War
Commanders	
Current commander	General He Yung-chien (何雍堅)

	**This article contains Chinese text.** Without proper rendering support, you may see question marks, boxes, or other symbols instead of Chinese characters.

The **Republic of China Military Police** (traditional Chinese: 中華民國憲兵; pinyin: *Zhōnghuá Mínguó Xiànbīng*) is a military police body under the Ministry of National Defense of the Republic of China (ROC). Unlike military police in many other countries, ROCMP is a separate branch of the ROC Armed Forces.

History

Warlords Era

The Republic of China Military Police dated back to 1914. When the provisional president of Republic of China, Dr. Sun Yat-sen, took the office in Guangzhou, an internal security unit was established to enforce military discipline among the troops loyal to the Republic of China Provisional Government. This unit was later renamed Military Police and would gradually expands and become present-day Republic of China Military Police. In 1925, under the supervision of then general Chiang Kai-shek, the military police was expanded from a single company to a full battalion, and was attached to the Northern Expedition Forces the next year. In the next ten years, the military police gradually expanded into several regiments, and was active in purging the communist elements within the Nationalist government.

Xi'an Incident

Main article: Xi'an Incident

On December 12, 1936, while accompanying Chiang Kai-shek on an inspection trip to Xi'an, members of Military Police clashed with Zhang Xueliang's elite bodyguards when the latter were sent to arrest the generalissimo. The military police were caught off guard and out numbered, and were soon overpowered by Zhang's force, who later arrested Chiang and his entourage in what is later known as the Xi'an Incident. More than one hundred military police became casualties in the brief battle. However, to commemorate the heroic actions of the Military Police, Chiang ordered December 12 to be the Military Police Day. This holiday is no longer observed by the Republic of China government.

World War Two and Civil War

Military Police during the January 28 Incident.

During the Second Sino-Japanese War, the Military Police troopers sometimes found themselves clashing with the Japanese despite the fact that they were neither properly trained nor equipped for such combat tasks. In the January 28 Incident, Shanghai and Battle of Nanjing in 1932 and 1937, the Military Police put up fierce resistance against the Japanese forces, and suffered heavy casualties. The

Military Police were also instrumental in operations behind Japanese line, and in time continued to expand under the direction of Nationalist Military. Military Police were also active in keeping the influences of the communists at bay, and were successful at quelling an attempted insurrection by the communists in 1941. The last task of the Military Police in the war was to provide escort to the Japanese delegates to arrange the surrender.

Full scale civil war broke out in 1946 between the Nationalists and the Communists; however, the Military Police were not as active in combat as they once were in the war against Japan. The Military Police were tasked to protect important governmental facilities from sabotages as well as political figures from assassinations. Furthermore, several Military Police regiments were involved in suppressing civil unrests in the newly acquired territories of Taiwan. The Military Police headquarters were moved to Taipei, Taiwan in 1950 following the defeat on mainland and evacuation to Taiwan.

Taiwan

In 1970, under the advice from the US Military Mission to the ROC, the ROC Armed Forces reorganized all their regiments into brigades. On 16 March 1970, the Military Police Command formed up four regional commands from the original military police regiments: 201st regional command from the 101st Military Police regiment for presidential guards, 202nd from the 201st MP regiment for capital garrison, 203rd from the 202nd MP regiment in Miaoli, and 204th from the 203rd MP regiment in Tainan City.

In January 2006, all ten security battalions under the Republic of China Air Force were transferred to the Military Police Command.

Functions

From the 2006 National Defense Report, Republic of China Military Police performs

1. Military functions:
    1. special security duties, including presidential protection,
    2. counter-terrorism operations,
    3. garrison security,
    4. enforce military discipline,
    5. support military operations,
2. Supportive functions in civilian affairs:
    1. execute military justice and law enforcement missions,
    2. maintain public security,
    3. adequately support regional disaster prevention,
    4. response, and ensure social stability and national security.

A military policeman on guard duty near the Cihu Presidential Burial Place, where Chiang Kai-shek is entombed.

Military

ROCMP is responsible for enforcing military law, maintaining military discipline, providing manpower support for the civilian police force, performing combat duty in times of emergency, providing security for certain governmental facilities such as including the Presidential Palace, and performing counter-terrorism and VIP protection operations. It is also responsible for the defense of Taipei, the capital city and political and financial center of the Republic of China.

Intelligence

Due to traditional and historical reasons, Republic of China Military Police still carry out intelligence missions in six categories of Security Investigations to fulfill its tasked functions:

- Special Services for presidential security and protection
- Politics
- Military
- Criminal Cases
- Foreign Affairs
- Social Order

These Security Investigations are mainly run by every regional investigation group, the mobile investigation group, and their superior unit: Intelligence Division of the Military Police Command. The main goal of these six Security Investigations is centered at the first one: Special Services for presidential security and protection. More practically, it is to satisfy the request from the Commander in Chiefs, the Taiwan President.

While performing its intelligence missions, Republic of China Military Police is submitted to the supervisory and coordination from National Security Bureau of National Security Council.

Law enforcement

In accordance with; Clause 2, Section 1 of Article 229; Clause 2, Section 1 of Article 230; and Clause 2, Section 1 of Article 231 of The Criminal Procedure Code of the ROC, the commissioned and non-commissioned officers, and the enlisted persons of the MP Corps have the authority to assist public prosecutors or to be commanded by prosecutors to investigate crime activities. In the other words, performing the authority of Judicial Police are given by The Criminal Procedure Code of the ROC to the Security MP troops in the regional Military Police units, and it is the same in nature as the polices performing the actual criminal investigations. Before the establishment and expansion of the mobile forces of special police corps in Taiwan, Military Police troops were the main force to secure and prevent high-profile criminal activities, heavy violence, and frequent society disorders or riots. At present, Military Police troops are still aggressively working with and commanded by the district public procurator systems to investigate criminal cases. The Security MP troops are still one of the important forces that uphold the law and order of society in Taiwan.

Because of the frequent military personnel rotations and the conscription system in the ROC, people within the regional Military Police units develop relatively fewer ties with local residents, in comparison with the local police departments. Also, the local police departments must answer to the corresponding local elected officials administratively but the regional Military Police units do not. In the cases of prostitution and human slavery, this makes the ROC Military Police the preferred law enforcement unit for the public prosecutors of all levels in Taiwan, because of minimal information leakage or less interference from domestic politicians.

In cases of fugitive recovery, some public prosecutors mobilize the military police to handle large-scale searches or arrests because military police can provide massive manpower with good discipline and fewer gang-related interpersonal relationships.

Organization

Military Police Command (憲兵司令部) is responsible for all Military Police units and operations. It is subordinate to the Armed Force General Staff, the Minister of National Defense, and the Republic of China President. It includes internal units that are responsible for political warfare, units inspection, personnel, intelligence, operation, logistics, and communication. It is also responsible for the following units and divisions:

- Military Police School (zh-tw:憲兵學校, ja:憲兵學校 (中華民國))
- Military Police Regional Commands (x4) (指揮部)
  - Military Police Armor Battalions (x2) (裝甲憲兵營)
  - Artillery Battalion (x1) (砲兵營)
  - Military Police Battalions (x19) (憲兵營)
  - Security Battalions (x10) (警衛營): Specially tasked to guard military air bases or field.
  - Regional Military Police Offices (x22) (憲兵隊): It is a battalion-size unit stationed in the urban area.
    - Regional Military Police Investigation Groups (憲兵調查組): Administratively, it belongs to its corresponding regional office; operationally, it is controlled by the intelligence division(G2) of the Military Police Command.
- Forensic Science Center (zh-tw:刑事鑑識中心)
  - Chemical Forensic Division (化學鑑識組)
  - Physical Forensic Division (物理鑑識組)
  - Crime Scene Investigation Division (現場勘查組)
- Military Police Special Services Company, MPSSC (zh-tw:憲兵特勤隊): Code-named **Night Hawk.**
- Sindian Military Prison, Taipei County (台北新店軍事監獄)
- Lioujia Military Prison, Tainan County (台南六甲軍事監獄)

Equipments

Military Police was the first branch to be issued with T91 assault rifles.

T75 pistols are the standard issued side-arms issued to all Military Police personnel.

Model	Origin
AM General Humvee	United States
CM-32 Armoured Vehicle	Taiwan
Harley-Davidson 883 Sportster	United States
V-150 APC	United States

Small arms

Model	Origin
AT4	United States
M2 QCB .50 heavy machine gun	United States
M24 Sniper Weapon System	United States
MK153 SMAW	United States
Mk 19 grenade launcher	United States

T74 machine gun	Taiwan
T75 Light machine gun	Taiwan
T75 pistols	Taiwan
T-77 Submachine gun	Taiwan
T-85 grenade launcher	Taiwan
T91 assault rifle	Taiwan

Fire support

Model	Origin
M120 120 mm mortar	United States
T-75 60mm mortar	Taiwan

See also

- Military of the Republic of China
- National Police Agency (Republic of China)

External references

- ROC Military Police Command [1] (Chinese (Taiwan))
- ROC Military Police Reservist Forum [2] (Chinese (Taiwan))

Chungshan Institute of Science and Technology

Chungshan Institute of Science and Technology

The **Chung-Shan Institute of Science and Technology** (中山科學研究院) is the primary research and development institution of the Republic of China Ministry of National Defense's Armaments Bureau and has been active in the development of various weapons systems and dual use technology. CSIST is also involved in developing systems for Taiwan's civilian space program. The institute is administered under the Armaments Bureau of the ROC Ministry of National Defense (MND), and is headquartered in Longtan Township, Taoyuan County, Taiwan.

History

CSIST was established by the Republic of China government in 1969 to serve as a military R&D and systems integration center Early work includes various missile and radar systems, as well as systems integration for ROC military aircraft and ships.

The institute was involved in several attempted nuclear weapons programs during the Cold War. In 1967, a nuclear weapons program began under the auspices of the Institute of Nuclear Energy Research (INER) of CIST. After the International Atomic Energy Agency found evidence of the ROC's efforts to produce weapons-grade plutonium, Taipei agreed in September 1976 under U.S. pressure to dismantle its nuclear weapons program. Though the nuclear reactor was soon shut down and the plutonium mostly returned to the U.S., a secret program was revealed when Colonel Chang, Hsien-yi, deputy director of nuclear research at INER, defected to the U.S. in December 1987 and produced a cache of incriminating documents. General Hau Pei-tsun claimed that scientists in Taiwan had already produced a controlled nuclear reaction. Presently there is no evidence that a nuclear weapons program is being pursued, and government officials have stated that Taiwan will not develop nuclear, chemical, or biological weapons.

The Institute expanded to the development of dual use technology in 1994. With the expansion of Taiwan's civilian space program, CSIST has also become involved in design of various satellite and launch systems, the latter of which have consisted primarily of scientific rockets to study the ionosphere.

Developed weapons systems

Fighter aircraft

- AIDC F-CK Indigenous Defence Fighter: Developed by division later spun off as AIDC and was a contractor also. Worked with AIDC to provide upgrades for the IDF.

Missiles

- Hsiung Feng I (HF-1): sea and ground based subsonic Anti-ship missile.
- Hsiung Feng II (HF-2): improved HF-1 with air-to-ground missile.
- Hsiung Feng IIE (HF-2E): land attack cruise missile system based on the HF-2
- Hsiung Feng III (HF-3): supersonic anti-ship missile currently in development
- Kun Wu 1 (KW 1): clone of the 9K11 Malyutka anti-tank missile, already phased out of ROCA service.
- Kung Feng 6 (KF 6): locally developed MLRS.
- Sky Bow I (TK-1): surface-to-air missile system.
- Sky Bow II (TK-2): advanced version of TK-1 with longer range and some anti-missile capability.
- Sky Bow III (TK-3): anti-ballistic missile system (partially based on Patriot-2 technology) - in development
- Sky Sword I (TC-1): IR guided air-to-air missile.
- Sky Sword II (TC-2): radar guided air-to-air missile.
- Thunderbolt-2000 (LT-2000): locally developed MLRS.

Organization

The institute is divided into six research divisions and four centers.

Research Divisions

- Aeronautical Systems
- Missile and Rocket Systems
- Information and Communications
- Chemical Systems
- Materials and Electro-Optics
- Electronic Systems

Centers

- System Development
- System Manufacturing
- Integrated Logistical Support
- Information Management

See also

- Military of the Republic of China
- National Space Organization (Taiwan ROC)
- Taiwan and weapons of mass destruction

External references

- CSIST website [1] (Chinese)

Conscription in the Republic of China

Conscription in the Republic of China

The **Republic of China (Taiwan)** has maintained a policy of **conscription** for all qualified males of military age since 1949, primarily as a means to bolster the defense of Taiwan against an invasion by the People's Republic of China. Females from the outlying islands of Fuchien, which are geographically closest to mainland China, were also required to serve in a civil defense role, although this requirement has been dropped since the lifting of martial law. Although the majority of all enlisted positions in the ROC Armed Forces have been and are currently filled by draftees, the government intends to gradually expand the number of volunteer soldiers with the eventual goal of forming an all volunteer military. However, even then there will be compulsory basic training for all males reaching 18. Recent years have also seen an increase in the service options open to draftees, including alternative service with the Ministry of the Interior (MOI), as well as specialized service options for draftees in specific professions. The draft process is set forth under the ROC Military Service Act under the auspices of the MOI's National Conscription Agency as well as by Article 20 of the ROC Constitution.

The ROC Defense Ministry had announced that should voluntary enlistment reach sufficient numbers, the compulsory service period for draftees will be shortened to 14 months in 2007. It will be further shortened to 12 months in 2009.

On March 10, 2009 Minister of Defence Chen Chao-min said by the end of 2014 Taiwan will have an all volunteer military force. The process of removing conscription will begin in 2010 and by the end of 2014 an all volunteer force will replace the conscipts. Individuals who wish to join must have a minimum of high school education and those who do not volunteer for the military will be forced to complete four months of military boot camp.

Should this policy remain unchanged, although Taiwan will have a purely volunteer professional force, every male will still be conscripted to receive a three to four month military training. Thus, after 2014, compulsory military service will still remain in practice in Taiwan.

Eligibility

18-22 years of age for selective compulsory military service, with 24-month service obligation; no minimum age for voluntary service (all officers are volunteers); 18-19 years of age for women high school graduates who meet requirements for specific military jobs (2009). Both men and women have been drafted. Under the current Military Service Act, all ROC citizens between the ages of 19 and 36 are considered to be of "draft age" and are subject to conscription, including those possessing dual citizenship (though the ROC does recognise dual citizenship). Generally, dual citizens who are males of military age are not permitted to renounce their ROC citizenship prior to completing their service obligations. Draftable males classified as Overseas Chinese are exempt from the draft provided they do not reside continuously in the Taiwan Area for a) more than four months at a time for those born in 1984 and before or b) more than 183 days in a two year period.

All draft age males will receive notices requiring them to report to the conscription sections of their local government offices at age 19 for preliminary assessment. Deferments are available for students of higher education institutions up to certain cutoff ages (24 for a bachelors degree, 27 for a masters degree, and 30 for a doctoral degree), as well as for draftees with one sibling already serving. Following completion of the active duty service period, all draftees are demobilized with all emigration restrictions lifted and are considered reservists until age 40.

Draft age males are subject to restrictions on leaving the country prior to fulfilling their service obligations and require approval from either their local district offices (for short term visits abroad), or the MOI Immigration Bureau for students attending institutions of higher education abroad.

Draft dodgers are subject to criminal charges.

Service options

The following compulsory service options are available as of January 2006:

- Enlisted military service (士兵役): 12 months of active duty enlisted military service in one of the four branches of the ROC Armed Forces.
- Alternative service (替代役): 12 months of public safety or community service related work under the MOI, usually in the police, fire department, public clinics, local government offices, or as teachers in rural areas. Various billets are available only to draftees with related qualifications.
- National defense service (國防役): Available to draftees with advanced degrees, particularly in the sciences and engineering, who upon selection, receive 3 months of officer training culminating in a commission as an officer in the reserves, followed by four years of employment in a government or academic research institution such as the Academia Sinica or Industrial Technology Research Institute.

Draft process

The military draft process occurs in four steps:

1. Military Registration Investigation: Interview conducted by the conscription sections of local government offices to determine the educational background of the draftee as well as any special skills (e.g. proficiency in a foreign language). Generally occurs upon a male ROC national's 19th birthday or periodically upon his establishment (or change) of residence in ROC administered territories while of draft age but not yet drafted. Education and other deferments may be granted at

this point if the draftee is eligible. If the draftee is not eligible for a deferment, a physical examination is scheduled. The draftee may also apply for alternative or national defense service at this point. In the case of the latter, the draftee will be required to compete successfully at an officer selection board for the desired billet, after which he will continue directly on to officer training school following completion of the physical exam.

2. Physical Examination: Draftee undergoes a full physical examination at a hospital approved by the Department of Health. Physical fitness is classified on three levels, A, B, and C, with level A and B draftees considered physically fit for military service.
3. Drawing Lots: Draftees fit for military service then draw lots to determine if they will serve in the Army, Navy, Air Force, or Marine Corps (Military police officers are selected from Army draftees). The chances of drawing for each service are not equal with the Army generally being the most probable, the Navy intermediate, and the Air Force and Marines being the least probable.
4. Basic Training: After being assigned a service branch, the draftee is then assigned a date to begin basic training, after which the draftee will enter active duty.

External links

- National Conscription Agency, Ministry of the Interior [1]
- Military draft information, Dept. of Compulsory Military Service, Taipei City Government [2]
- Conscription Information, Ministry of National Defense [3] (archived from the original [4] on 2006-11-27)

National Sports Training Center football team

National Sports Training Center football team

Full name	National Sports Training Center football team
Founded	1960
Chairman	Chang Chia-kuang (張家廣)
Manager	Wang Chia-chung (王家中)
League	Enterprise Football League
2007	2nd
Home colours	**Away colours**

The **National Sports Training Center (NSTC) football team** is the football team in Taiwan's National Sports Training Center. It was merged in 2003 with the Lukuang football team, Taiwan's land army football team, after the option of alternate service in the Taiwanese militia. It participates in Taiwan's Enterprise Football League

History

Formerly known as the **Lukuang football team** (Chinese: 陸光足球隊; pinyin: *Lùguāng zúqiúduì*) or **Taiwan Army football team**, the NTSC football team belonged to the Republic of China Army and competed in the Chinese Taipei National Football League.

Since the Republic of China has the policy of conscription for all male citizens, qualified footballers could choose to join the Lukuang football team instead of the regular militia service after passing the tryouts. It helped the players to keep their form and provided additional selection and management to the Chinese Taipei national football team. As a result, most national team members have played for Lukuang.

In 2000, Lukuang quit the league due to military reform, but returned in 2003 under the new name of **Taiwan National Sports Training Center football team** and are affiliated with Taiwan's National Sports Training Center.

Naming Scheme

The Taiwan NSTC football team team enters the Enterprise Football League with a different name every year.

- 2006: Fubon Financial (富邦金控)
- 2007: Kenting Chateau (墾丁夏都)
- 2008: National Sports Training Center

Current squad

Note: Flags indicate national team as has been defined under FIFA eligibility rules. Players may hold more than one non-FIFA nationality.

No.		Position	Player
1		GK	Hung Tsung-cheng*
2		DF	Wang Chih-sheng
3		MF	Feng Pao-hsing
4		DF	Lin Yu-te*
5		DF	Lu Tu-ming*
6		MF	Wang Yong-lun
7		MF	Tsai Chih-chieh
8		MF	Wu Ku-feng
9		MF	Tseng Tai-lin
10		MF	Lin Tsung-jen
11		DF	Chen Chang-min*
12		DF	Lin Cheng-yi*
13		MF	Huang Kuan-jen*
14		DF	Chen Chun-chieh

No.		Position	Player
15		DF	Huang Jui-ying*
16		MF	Chen Meng-hsien*
17		DF	Chen Chien-hung*
20		MF	Ko Hung-chi
21		MF	Fang Ching-jen
23		FW	Wang Cheng-ming*
24		MF	Chang Fu-hsiang
25		MF	Huang Yen-wei*
26		MF	Huang Shih-chan*
27		FW	Chen Bing-shin
28		FW	Tai Yu-che*
29		MF	Pan Wei-hung*
30		GK	Pan Wei-chih

** Name spellings of some players have yet been confirmed. See zh:*台灣國訓足球隊 *for their Chinese names.*

Recent transfers

In

- Tsai Chih-chieh
- Wang Chih-sheng
- Wang Yong-lun

Out

- Chen Chi-feng *(to Taipower)*
- Chuang Wei-lun *(to Tatung)*
- Hsu Jen-feng *(to Tatung)*
- Lee Meng-chian *(to Taipower)*
- Liang Chien-wei *(to Taipower)*
- Lin Po-yuan *(to Taipower)*

Achievements

As Lukuang

- **Chinese Taipei National Football League:**
    - **Runners-up (2):** 1984, 1991

As NSTC

- **Chinese Taipei National Football League:**
    - **Runners-up (1):** 2007

Managers

- Jong Chien-wu (鍾劍武), 1991

See also

- Conscription in the Republic of China
- Military of the Republic of China

Tri-Service General Hospital

Tri-Service General Hospital

President	Dah-Shyong You, Major General (于大雄)
Type	Medical center
Established	1946
Location	Taipei, Republic of China

The **Tri-Service General Hospital** (Chinese: 三軍總醫院; pinyin: *Sānjūn Zǒngyīyuàn*; abbreviation **TSGH**) is a medical center in Taipei, Republic of China. It is the teaching hospital of the National Defense Medical Center.

External links

- Tri-Service General Hospital [1]
- National Defense Medical Center [2]

Guningtou War Museum

The **Guningtou War Museum** or **Kuningtou Battle Museum** (Chinese: 古寧頭戰史館) is located in the Kuningtou area of the Kinmen National Park, Kinmen County, Fujian Province, Republic of China (Taiwan). It was built in 1984 to commemorate the Battle of Guningtou (started in 1949 and extended through the 1950s) between the Republic of China and the communist People's Republic of China.

External links

- Kinmen's Guningtou area attractions commemorate important battle [1]
- 中華民國博物館學會 - 古寧頭戰史館 [2]

Republic of China Army rank insignia

Republic of China Army rank insignia

Rank Structure

The rank system of the Republic of China Army is based on Wehrmacht during the Sino-Germany cooperation era. Currently, the rank structure is getting closer to the one used by the United States Army.

Commissioned Officers

Title	Second Lieutenant 少尉	First Lieutenant 中尉	Captain 上尉
Insignia			

Title	Major 少校	Lieutenant Colonel 中校	Colonel 上校
Insignia			

Title	Brigadier General 少將	Major General 中將	Lieutenant General 二級上將	General 一級上將
Insignia				

Non-Commissioned Officers

Title	Corporal 下士	Sergeant 中士	Staff Sergeant 上士	Sergeant First Class 三等士官長	Master Sergeant 二等士官長	Sergeant Major 一等士官長
Insignia						

Enlisted Personnel

Title	Private E-1 二等兵	Private E-2 一等兵	Private First Class 上等兵
Insignia			

References

- The International Encyclopedia of Uniform Insignia around the World [1]

2007 Hukou F-5F crash

2007 Hukou F-5F crash

Location of Hukou, Hsinchu	
Accident summary	
Date	11 May 2007
Type	Under investigation
Site	Hukou, Taiwan
Passengers	0
Crew	2
Injuries	8 (on the ground)
Fatalities	5 (including 3 on the ground)
Survivors	0
Aircraft type	Northrop F-5
Operator	Republic of China Air Force
Tail number	5371

A Republic of China Air Force F-5F fighter jet **crashed into a military base in Hukou** (湖口), Taiwan on 11 May 2007. The accident killed the two Taiwanese crewmen and three Singaporean soldiers who were part of an unrelated unilateral training stint on the ground. Another eight Singaporeans were injured, with one sustaining serious burn injuries.

Han Kuang exercise

The fighter jet, designation ROCAF F-5F 5371, was conducting a training flight in a rehearsal for Taiwan's Han Kuang 23 military exercise (漢光演習) in the following week. The twin-seat fighter jet took off with three other aircraft from an airbase in Taitung County; it crashed 30 minutes later during a simulated low-altitude attack while executing an "anti-parachuting" drill.

Crash at military base

At 9.38am, the fighter jet crashed at Hukou Army Base about 50 km southwest of the capital Taipei. The base houses the 542nd Armour Brigade of the 6th Army Corps, Republic of China Army, it also hosts a visiting training detachment from the Singapore Armed Forces (SAF). Eyewitnesses say the F-5F aircraft failed to pull up in time, and crashed into the base.

The Taiwan Ministry of National Defense reported that the pilot apparently attempted to steer the plane away from residential area before crashing into a storeroom within the military compound where the Singapore detachment was stationed. Several soldiers were in the storeroom at that time.

Due to the lack of space in Singapore, the island state has been conducting unilateral military training in Taiwan as part of a cooperative agreement. Singapore is not involved in the Han Kuang exercise.

Casualties

The accident killed five people. The two crewmen and another two soldiers on the ground were killed during the initial crash. Another soldier subsequently succumbed to his wounds 17 days later. The Taiwanese crewmen are pilot Major Wei Tzu-yuan (魏子淵), age 34, and co-pilot Captain Chan Chia-chun (詹嘉鈞), age 27. They had 1500 and 700 hours of flight experience respectively. They belong to the 45 Fighter Squadron, 737 Tactical Fighter Wing, Republic of China Air Force, based in Taitung Airbase.

The initial two Singaporean fatalities are 3rd Sergeant Isz Sazli Bin Sapari, age 19, and Private Fan Yao Jin, age 23. Both were full-time national servicemen (NSFs). The third fatality is Lance Corporal Chow Han Min Calvin, age 19. LCP Chow had 50 per cent body surface burns and respiratory burns, and was airlifted back to Singapore for further treatment. However, LCP Chow's condition worsened and he died in the Singapore General Hospital on 28 May 2007 at 6.37am.

One Singapore soldier remains critically injured. 23-year-old 3rd Sergeant Ramakrishnan Karthigayan from the 6th Battalion, Singapore Infantry Regiment (6 SIR) suffered 45 percent total body surface area burns. He, along with LCP Chow, was treated at the Taoyuan Tri-service General Hospital before being evacuated to Singapore on 12 May to receive treatment at the Singapore General Hospital Burns Centre. As of May 2007, Ramakrishnan remains in a critical but stable condition. Seven other Singaporeans had minor injuries and received outpatient treatment.

Investigation

The cause of the crash has not yet been determined. Taiwan local media pointed out that the age of the F-5F fleet as a possible factor. The Ministry of Defense announced that it has grounded all F-5F fighters, pending the outcome of an investigation into the accident.

The F5E and F5F fighter jets were developed by Northrop in the United States in the 1960s. In the 1970s, Taiwan produced about 300 of the jets; about 90 are still in service in Taiwan.

The Singapore Ministry of Defence announced that it is also conducting an investigation of the incident.

According to *United Daily News*, pilot Wei was last heard shouting "Up!" before the accident occurred. Due to security reasons, radio communication was minimized during the exercise. The aircraft did not have a flight data recorder (black box), but was equipped with Air Combat Maneuvering Instrumentation (ACMI) that could be useful in the investigation.

Preliminary findings

On 14 May 2007, air force major-general Liu Chen-wu released preliminary findings of the investigation at the Legislative Yuan. He said that during the simulated attack, the fighter jet had deviated from its planned route. In his effort to lock in to ground targets, the pilot might have flown too low. The pilot chose not to eject in order to steer the plane away from built up areas and avoid heavy casualties. Liu said that they "chose to sacrifice their lives and divert the plane to the military compound." He did not rule out mechanical problems causing the aircraft to be stalled because the pilot could have pulled out safely if he had activated maximum power and afterburner.

There are reports that visibility was low at Hukou during the exercise.

Aftermath

A day after the incident, Su Tseng-chang, the premier of the Republic of China, ordered the air force to speed up an overhaul of warplanes. He made the order just before announcing his resignation following his defeat in the ruling Democratic Progressive Party's primary to pick a candidate for the Republic of China presidential election, 2008.

Taiwan Ministry of National Defense (MND) announced that the five-day Han Kuang exercise would be carried out as scheduled despite the crash. This prompted legislator Hsueh Ling to call for defense minister Lee Jye to step down.

Related incidents

Legislator Hsueh noted that seventeen F-5E/F jet fighters have been lost in accidents since 1988.

External links

- Pre-accident pictures of the airplane [1]
- News report with pictures [2] - Apple Daily (Taiwan) (Chinese)

Wei (rank)

Wei (rank)

Wei (尉) is the rank held by company-grade officers in the military of both the People's Republic of China and the Republic of China. It currently exists in three grades, **Shao Wei** (少尉), **Zhong Wei** (中尉) (**Chung Wei** using Wade-Giles), and **Shang Wei** (上尉). An additional grade, **Da Wei** (大尉), formerly existed in the People's Liberation Army, during the period 1955-1965. However when the use of rank and insignia was restored in 1988, this rank was not reestablished. As opposed to the Western tradition of using different names for equivalent ranks in the Army and Navy, Chinese armed forces use the same rank names for all services, prefixed in the case of the PLA by Hai Jun (海军) (Naval Force) or Kong Jun (空军) (Air Force).

Rank	Literal translation	Army translation	Navy translation	ROC Army insignia	NATO rank equivalent
Da Wei (大尉) (used only 1955-1965 by PLA)	Grand Officer	Senior Captain	Captain Lieutenant	N/A	OF-2
Shang Wei (上尉)	Senior Officer	Captain	Lieutenant		
Zhong Wei (中尉) (Chung Wei)	Middle Officer	First Lieutenant	Sub-Lieutenant		OF-1
Shao Wei (少尉)	Junior Officer	Second Lieutenant	Ensign		

See also

- Ranks of the People's Liberation Army
- Ranks of the People's Liberation Army Navy
- Ranks of the People's Liberation Army Air Force
- Republic of China Armed Forces rank insignia

Xiao (rank)

Xiao (rank)

Xiao (校) (Wade-Giles: **Hsiao**) is the rank held by field officers in the military of both the People's Republic of China and the Republic of China. The People's Liberation Army uses four grades while the Republic of China uses only three, with the rank equivalent to the fourth being treated as a general officer rank. This difference is found in other militaries as well. For example. in the British Army a brigadier is considered a field officer, while the equivalent rank in the United States Army, brigadier general, is considered a general officer. The PLA use the same rank names for all services, prefixed by Hai Jun (海军) (Naval Force) or Kong Jun (空军) (Air Force). While the ROC does the same for enlisted ranks and company-grade officers, it has distinct names for the higher naval ranks.

Rank	Literal translation	Army translation	Navy translation	PLA Naval Force insignia	PLA Air Force insignia	ROC Army insignia	NATO rank equivalent
Da Xiao (大校)	Grand Field Officer	Brigadier	Commodore			N/A	OF-6
Shang Xiao (上校) (Shang Hsiao)	Senior Field Officer	Colonel	Captain				OF-5
Zhong Xiao (中校) (Chung Hsiao)	Middle Field Officer	Lieutenant Colonel	Commander				OF-4
Shao Xiao (少校) (Shao Hsiao)	Junior Field Officer	Major	Lieutenant Commander				OF-3

See also

- Ranks of the People's Liberation Army
- Ranks of the People's Liberation Army Navy
- Ranks of the People's Liberation Army Air Force
- Republic of China Armed Forces rank insignia

Jiang (rank)

Jiang (rank)

Jiang (将) (Wade-Giles: **Chiang**; traditional Chinese: 將) is the rank held by general officers in the military of both the People's Republic of China and the Republic of China. The People's Liberation Army uses three grades at present while the Republic of China uses four, with the rank equivalent to the fourth being treated as a field officer rank in the PLA (i.e. Senior Colonel equivalent to Brigadier General and to ROC's 少将 Major General). This difference is found in other militaries as well. For example. in the British Army a brigadier is considered a field officer, while the equivalent rank in the United States Army, brigadier general, is considered a general officer. The PLA uses the same rank names for all services, prefixed by Hai Jun (海军) (Naval Force) or Kong Jun (空军) (Air Force). While the ROC does the same for enlisted ranks and company-grade officers, it has distinct names for the higher naval ranks. Because of the additional field officer rank in the PLA, ranks with the same Chinese name do not correspond to the same rank. A similar situation occurs in the militaries of North and South Korea with some ranks.

People's Liberation Army

Rank	Literal translation	Army translation	Navy translation	PLA Ground Force insignia	PLA Naval Force insignia	PLA Air Force insignia	NATO rank equivalent
Yi Ji Shang Jiang (一级上将) Rank existed only 1988-1994; never held	First Class Senior General	General of the Army	Fleet Admiral				OF-10
Shang Jiang (上将)	Senior General	General	Admiral				OF-9
Zhong Jiang (中将)	Middle General	Lieutenant General	Vice Admiral				OF-8
Shao Jiang (少将)	Junior General	Major General	Rear Admiral				OF-7

Da Jiang

Under the rank system in place in the PLA in the era 1955-1965, there existed the rank of Da Jiang (大将) or Marshal. This rank was awarded to 10 of the veteran leaders of the PLA in 1955 and never conferred again. It was considered equivalent to the Soviet rank of Генера́л а́рмии (General of the Army) which is generally considered a five-star rank, although the insignia itself had only four. The decision to name the equivalent rank Yi Ji Shang Jiang when it was briefly reestablished in 1988-1994 was likely due to a desire to keep the rank of Da Jiang an honorary one awarded after a war, much as General of the Armies in the United States Army.

Republic of China Army

Insignia adopted in 1959. Rank names are given using Wade-Giles transliteration and traditional Chinese characters.

Rank	Army translation	Navy translation	ROC Army insignia	NATO rank equivalent
I Chi Shang Chiang (一級上將)	General 1st Class	Admiral 1st Class		OF-9
Er Chi Shang Chiang (二級上將)	General	Admiral		OF-8
Chung Chiang (中將)	Lieutenant General	Vice Admiral		OF-7
Shao Chiang (少將)	Major General	Rear Admiral		OF-6

See also

- Ranks of the People's Liberation Army
- Ranks of the People's Liberation Army Navy
- Ranks of the People's Liberation Army Air Force
- Republic of China Armed Forces rank insignia

References

- PLA Uniforms and Insignia [1]
- Military ranks of the People's Liberation Army [2]
- Military ranks of the People's Liberation Army Navy [3]
- Military ranks of the People's Liberation Army Air Force [4]
- Military ranks of the Army of the Republic of China [1]

Peiping National Military Council

Peiping National Military Council

Peiping National Military Council was the Republic of China's supreme military command in charge of the National Revolutionary Army forces in Northern China in the 1930s prior to the beginning of the Second Sino-Japanese War. As its name implies it was located in Peiping.

National Revolutionary Martyrs' Shrine

National Revolutionary Martyrs' Shrine

Geographical coordinates: 25°4′49.65″N 121°31′57.91″E

National Revolutionary Martyrs' Shrine	
Republic of China	
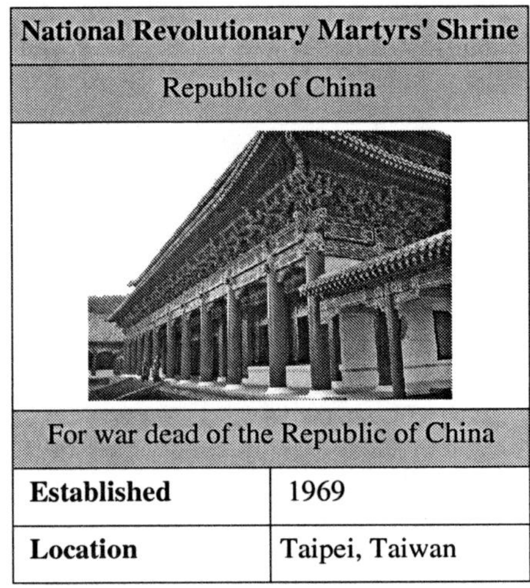	
For war dead of the Republic of China	
Established	1969
Location	Taipei, Taiwan

The **National Revolutionary Martyrs' Shrine** (國民革命忠烈祠) is a shrine in Taipei City, Taiwan, dedicated to the war dead of the Republic of China.

Built on Chingshan Mountain and overseeing the Keelung River in Taipei's Zhongshan District in 1969, the Martyrs Shrine recalls the architecture of the Hall of Supreme Harmony in Beijing's Forbidden City. The structure houses the spirit tablets of about 390,000 persons killed, among other engagements, during the Xinhai Revolution, Northern Expedition, Second Sino-Japanese War, Chinese Civil War, and the First and Second Taiwan Strait Crises. A changing of the honor guard from the various branches of the Republic of China Military, similar to the rituals at the Sun Yat-sen Memorial Hall and Chiang Kai-shek Memorial Hall, take place at the shrine.

The Martyrs' Shrine was the site of the funeral of Chiang Ching-kuo in 1988. On March 29 (Youth Day, commemorating the Huanghuagang Uprising) and September 3 (Armed Forces Day) of every year the President of the Republic of China leads the heads of the five Yuans (branches of government) to pay their respects to the martyrs by bowing and offering incense. Similar shrines are located in each locality in Taiwan, and similar ceremonies are led by county magistrates and city mayors.

Although the Martyrs Shrine is located in Taiwan, most of the soldiers honored served China and were born in Chinese provinces. Taiwan was ruled by Japan throughout World War II; its native soldiers served in the Japanese Imperial Army.

Front Gate.

Changing of the Guard.

Wu Yun An

Wu Yun An

This is a Chinese name; the family name is Wu.

Wu Yun An or **Yun-An Wu** (Chinese: 吳雲庵, October 25, 1897 - April 18, 1993) was a Chinese doctor, a Major General in the Chinese Army and Deputy Surgeon General of the Republic of China from 1945 to 1947, under Gen. Dr. Robert Kho-Seng Lim. In addition, from 1926 to 1928, Dr. Wu was head of public health at Whampoa Military Academy (Chinese: 黃埔軍校).

Dr. Wu graduated from Church Missionary Society Kwang Chi Medical School (Chinese: 大英廣濟醫學專門學校) in 1919 with degrees in clinical medicine (MB, ChB).

See also

- List of Christian Hospitals in China

External links

- Yun-An Wu, memoir archive, University of Heidelberg, Institute of Chinese Studies (Universität Heidelberg, Institut für Sinologie) [1]

Heng Shan Military Command Center

Heng Shan Military Command Center

Heng Shan Military Command Center (衡山指揮所) is an emergency military command center in Taiwan similar to Cheyenne Mountain in the United States. It is designed to withstand a 20 kilo-ton nuclear blast, a 2 kilo-ton conventional bombing and also EM pulse in event of an attack .The command center was constructed in 1978. The command is equipped with fiber optics, emergency power generators, and water supply. The base mainframe also has state-of-the-art tactical simulation system, Joint Theater Level Simulation (JTLS) from the United States military. The base is located in the heart of Dazhi Ya Nan mountain (大直) of Taipei City and is connected to the Yuan Shan Military Command Center (圓山指揮所) through a tunnel.

External links

- USJFCOM: Joint Theater Level Simulation (JTLS) [1]

Eternal Spring Shrine

Eternal Spring Shrine

Eternal Spring Shrine (also *Changchun Shrine*, *Chanchun Shrine*; simplified Chinese: 长春祠; traditional Chinese: 長春祠; pinyin: *Chángchūn cí*; literally "Ancestral shrine of Eternal, or Long, Spring"; 24°9′40.07″N 121°36′8.03″E) is a landmark and a memorial shrine complex in Taroko National Park in Taiwan, in Hualian County near town of Xiulin. It is one of the major picturesque points of the park, with the view of the mountains and the waterfall, and one of the main memorials for veterans.

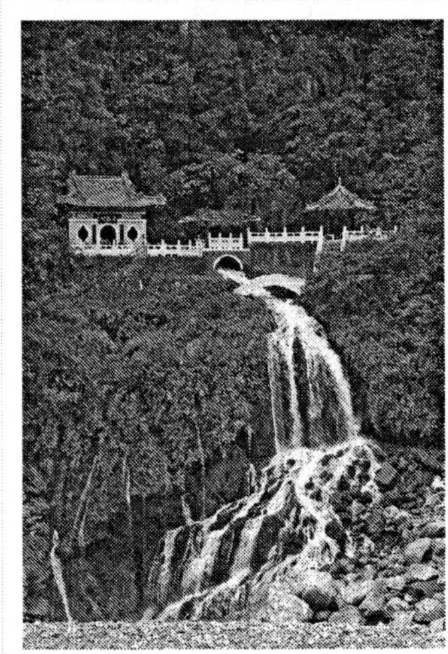

It was planned for construction in 1958 while the Central Cross-Island Highway was built nearby. It commemorates the memory of 212 veterans who died while constructing the Highway (1956—1960).

The name of the temple comes from the Changchun Falls that never stop running. The Shrine is located right above the waterfall streams.

Voice of Han

Voice of Han

Geographical coordinates: 25°2′14.46″N 121°31′16.91″E

Type	Radio network
Branding	VOH
Country	Taiwan
Availability	National, through regional substations.
Owner	Ministry of National Defense (Republic of China)
Launch date	1942
Former names	Military Radio
Official Website	Voice of Han [1]

Voice of Han Broadcasting Station (traditional Chinese: 漢聲廣播電台; pinyin: *hànshēng guǎngbō diàntái*) also known as **Voice of Han Chinese Broadcasting Station** was founded in 1942 by the Republic of China Ministry of National Defense. It is headquartered on Xinyi Road in the Zhongzheng District of Taipei, Taiwan. It's online broadcasting service and website are currently blocked in Mainland China.

History

1942, Voice of Han Radio was located in Mainland China and originally called Military Radio.

1949, the military radio station moved to Taiwan when the Kuomintang retreated following the Chinese Civil War.

1988, the military radio station was renamed to "Voice of Han" and launched more extensive coverage which offered listeners radio programs to listeners nationwide.

2002, on the 60th anniversary celebration of the radio station, President of the Republic of China, Chen Shui-bian broadcast a speech on Voice of Han calling for a communication bride between the two sides of the Taiwan Strait.

2010, Voice of Han Broadcasting in Kinmen added an additional frequency coverage, including Xiamen, which is located in Mainland China.

Frequency

FM

- Northern FM106.5 MHz (Hsinchu, Taoyuan, Taipei and Keelung)
- Central FM104.5 MHz (Hsinchu, Taichung, Nantou)
- Chang Southwest Region FM101.3 MHz (Changhua, Yunlin, Chiayi, Tainan)
- Kaohsiung-Pingtung area FM107.3 MHz (Kaohsiung, Pingtung)
- Taitung FM105.3 MHz
- Hualien FM104.5 MHz
- Yuli, FM107.3 MHz
- Ilan broadcast station FM106.5 MHz
- Kinmen relay station FM107.3 MHz

AM

- Taipei AM684/1116 kHz
- Taichung AM1287 kHz
- Taoyuan AM693/936 kHz
- Yunlin AM1089 kHz
- Tainan AM693 kHz
- Pingtung AM1332 kHz
- Hualien AM1359/792 kHz
- Ilan AM1116 kHz
- Penghu AM1269/846 kHz

Shortwave and Mediumwave

The Voice of Han also broadcasts propaganda programs to Mainland China on shortwave and mediumwave frequencies under the callsign "Voice of Guanghua" (光華之聲). Major programs include: Taiwan New Paradise, Music, Guanghua News, Guanghua Talk Forum, Culture and Education Filling Station, Two sides of the Taiwan Strait, Freedom Scene, Literature Bridge, Taiwan Strait Flyover, and Lookout Tower.

- Mainland China- 801 kHz 846 kHz 711 kHz 981 kHz 9745 kHz 1605 kHz

See also

- Propaganda in the Republic of China
- Media in Taiwan

External links

- Voice of Han(Traditional Chinese) [1]
- Voice of Guanghua(Simplified Chinese) [2]

Republic of China Armed Forces Museum

Republic of China Armed Forces Museum

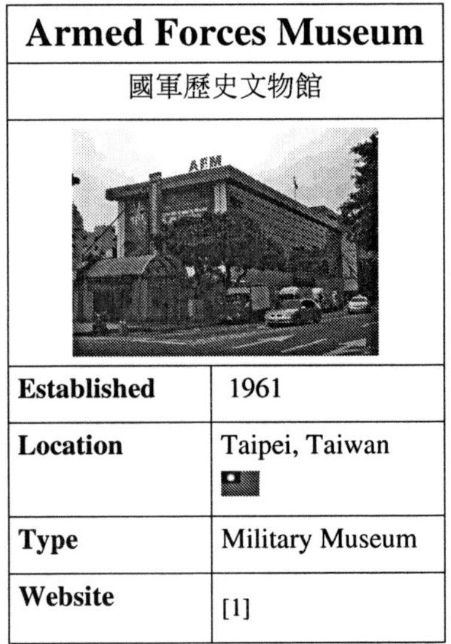

Armed Forces Museum	
國軍歷史文物館	
Established	1961
Location	Taipei, Taiwan
Type	Military Museum
Website	[1]

The **Republic of China Armed Forces Museum** (國軍歷史文物館) is located on Guiyang Street in the Poai District of Taipei in the Republic of China. It opened on October 31, 1961 under the administration of the Republic of China Ministry of National Defense Departmenf of History and Translation Office. The Museum aims to show the ROC military heritage of different periods and inform the public about the military. The museum encompasses 3 floors.

Permanent Exhibits

- From the Whampoa Army to the Northern Army
- Early Grueiling years in the War of Resistance - Features captured Japanese Military equipment including swords used during the Nanjing Massacre's Contest to kill 100 people using a sword.
- Counter Insurgency and Battle of the Taiwan Strait
- Modernization of the Military
- Weapons Collection Room.

Controversy

In 1999, a Taiwanese schoolgirl, Chang Fu-chen was raped and murdered at the Armed Forces Museum. Taipei Police found the girl's body dumped in a suburban Taipei park following the confession of Kuo Ching-ho, a military guard at the museum who was serving his conpulsory two-year military service.

See also

- Military Museum of the Chinese People's Revolution
- National Museum of History

External

Armed Forces Museum [2]

Order of National Glory

Order of National Glory

The **Order of National Glory** is the highest military award of the Republic of China Armed Forces, the army of the Republic of China. It was established on November 8, 1937.

Fuxing Broadcasting Station

Fuxing Broadcasting Station

Geographical coordinates: 25°5′13.15″N 121°31′41.63″E

Type	Radio network
Branding	Voice of Revival
Country	Taiwan
Availability	National, through regional substations.
Owner	Ministry of National Defense (Republic of China)
Launch date	1956
Official Website	Fuxing Radio [1]

Fuxing Broadcasting Station (traditional Chinese: 復興廣播電台; pinyin: *fùxìng guǎngbō diàntái*) is a radio station located on the campus of Ming Chuan University in Taipei, Taiwan and is operated by the Republic of China Ministry of National Defense. It's website is currently blocked in the People's Republic of China.

History and Overview

Fuxing Radio was founded on August 1, 1956 with units in Taipei, Taichung, and Kaohsiung. The station currently operates two radio networks. The first network acts as a "cross-strait" information service for domestic audiences. The second network and a shortwave network provides mainland chinese audiences with propaganda about Taiwan and the Republic of China.

Frequency

Taipei

- AM558, 909 kHz, the second radio network: AM594, 1089 kHz

Taichung

- FM107.8 MHz second radio network: AM594, 1089 kHz

Kaohsiung

- AM594 kHz, the second radio network: AM846 kHz

Mainland China

- HF Net: 9410,9774,15375 kHz

See Also

- Media in Taiwan
- Propaganda in the Republic of China

External Links

- Fuxing Radio [1]
- Voice of Fuxing [2]

Article Sources and Contributors

Republic of China Armed Forces *Source*: http://en.wikipedia.org/?oldid=390447841 *Contributors*: Bryan TMF

Whampoa Military Academy *Source*: http://en.wikipedia.org/?oldid=389653303 *Contributors*: McCaster

National Revolutionary Army *Source*: http://en.wikipedia.org/?oldid=390360120 *Contributors*: Asiaticus

Republic of China Military Academy *Source*: http://en.wikipedia.org/?oldid=389653044 *Contributors*: McCaster

Republic of China and weapons of mass destruction *Source*: http://en.wikipedia.org/?oldid=381412211 *Contributors*: 1 anonymous edits

Wuchih Mountain Military Cemetery *Source*: http://en.wikipedia.org/?oldid=383717513 *Contributors*: Rich Farmbrough

Republic of China Military Police *Source*: http://en.wikipedia.org/?oldid=377731471 *Contributors*: 1 anonymous edits

Chungshan Institute of Science and Technology *Source*: http://en.wikipedia.org/?oldid=356500975 *Contributors*: 1 anonymous edits

Conscription in the Republic of China *Source*: http://en.wikipedia.org/?oldid=377761298 *Contributors*: 1 anonymous edits

National Sports Training Center football team *Source*: http://en.wikipedia.org/?oldid=330978673 *Contributors*:

Tri-Service General Hospital *Source*: http://en.wikipedia.org/?oldid=344132363 *Contributors*: Borgarde

Guningtou War Museum *Source*: http://en.wikipedia.org/?oldid=373614229 *Contributors*: Iesvs.rex

Republic of China Army rank insignia *Source*: http://en.wikipedia.org/?oldid=344248108 *Contributors*: Carolina wren

2007 Hukou F-5F crash *Source*: http://en.wikipedia.org/?oldid=380730804 *Contributors*:

Wei (rank) *Source*: http://en.wikipedia.org/?oldid=389453509 *Contributors*:

Xiao (rank) *Source*: http://en.wikipedia.org/?oldid=375109786 *Contributors*: DM Zane

Jiang (rank) *Source*: http://en.wikipedia.org/?oldid=364603405 *Contributors*: 1 anonymous edits

Peiping National Military Council *Source*: http://en.wikipedia.org/?oldid=332373771 *Contributors*: R'n'B

National Revolutionary Martyrs' Shrine *Source*: http://en.wikipedia.org/?oldid=388686353 *Contributors*: Meiguoren

Wu Yun An *Source*: http://en.wikipedia.org/?oldid=382337976 *Contributors*: Epbr123

Heng Shan Military Command Center *Source*: http://en.wikipedia.org/?oldid=311613647 *Contributors*: Light.tebt

Eternal Spring Shrine *Source*: http://en.wikipedia.org/?oldid=344165568 *Contributors*: Fred Hsu

Voice of Han *Source*: http://en.wikipedia.org/?oldid=390074714 *Contributors*: Meiguoren

Republic of China Armed Forces Museum *Source*: http://en.wikipedia.org/?oldid=367735808 *Contributors*: Denglong

Order of National Glory *Source*: http://en.wikipedia.org/?oldid=376939700 *Contributors*: Pink Bull

Fuxing Broadcasting Station *Source*: http://en.wikipedia.org/?oldid=390218142 *Contributors*: Meiguoren

Image Sources, Licenses and Contributors

File:ROCN kang ding class.jpg *Source*: http://en.wikipedia.org/w/index.php?title=File:ROCN_kang_ding_class.jpg *License*: Public Domain *Contributors*: ROCN (Republic of China Navy)

File:Republic of China Army Flag.svg *Source*: http://en.wikipedia.org/w/index.php?title=File:Republic_of_China_Army_Flag.svg *License*: Public Domain *Contributors*: AnonMoos, Arilang1234, Fry1989, Homo lupus, Jusjih, Kibinsky, Mattes, Ms2ger, O, Odder, Permjak, Shibo77, Skipjack, Zscout370

File:Naval Jack of the Republic of China.svg *Source*: http://en.wikipedia.org/w/index.php?title=File:Naval_Jack_of_the_Republic_of_China.svg *License*: Public Domain *Contributors*: User:Zscout370

File:Flag of the United States.svg *Source*: http://en.wikipedia.org/w/index.php?title=File:Flag_of_the_United_States.svg *License*: Public Domain *Contributors*: User:Dbenbenn, User:Indolences, User:Jacobolus, User:Technion, User:Zscout370

File:Flag of France.svg *Source*: http://en.wikipedia.org/w/index.php?title=File:Flag_of_France.svg *License*: Public Domain *Contributors*: User:SKopp, User:SKopp, User:SKopp, User:SKopp, User:SKopp, User:SKopp

File:Flag of Germany.svg *Source*: http://en.wikipedia.org/w/index.php?title=File:Flag_of_Germany.svg *License*: Public Domain *Contributors*: User:Madden, User:Pumbaa80, User:SKopp

File:Flag of the United Kingdom.svg *Source*: http://en.wikipedia.org/w/index.php?title=File:Flag_of_the_United_Kingdom.svg *License*: Public Domain *Contributors*: User:Zscout370

File:IDF F-CK-1A Single Front View.jpg *Source*: http://en.wikipedia.org/w/index.php?title=File:IDF_F-CK-1A_Single_Front_View.jpg *License*: Creative Commons Attribution-Sharealike 2.5 *Contributors*: 王常松 Chang-Song Wang

Image:Chinese soldiers 1939.jpg *Source*: http://en.wikipedia.org/w/index.php?title=File:Chinese_soldiers_1939.jpg *License*: Public Domain *Contributors*: Original uploader was Jiang at en.wikipedia. Later version(s) were uploaded by Arilang1234 at en.wikipedia.

Image:ROCN Guard Martyrs Shrine.jpg *Source*: http://en.wikipedia.org/w/index.php?title=File:ROCN_Guard_Martyrs_Shrine.jpg *License*: Public Domain *Contributors*: User:Changlc

File:Zhongwen.svg *Source*: http://en.wikipedia.org/w/index.php?title=File:Zhongwen.svg *License*: Public Domain *Contributors*: AnonMoos, Asoer, Hämbörger, King of Hearts, Kjoonlee, Rjanag, 6 anonymous edits

File:1924 Emblem of Chinese Military Academy designed by Sun Yat-sen.gif *Source*: http://en.wikipedia.org/w/index.php?title=File:1924_Emblem_of_Chinese_Military_Academy_designed_by_Sun_Yat-sen.gif *License*: Public Domain *Contributors*: Sun Yat-sen

File:Republic China Army flag.gif *Source*: http://en.wikipedia.org/w/index.php?title=File:Republic_China_Army_flag.gif *License*: Public Domain *Contributors*: 1893 Chinese revolutionary Luk Howtung (陸皓東)

File:Whampoa3.jpg *Source*: http://en.wikipedia.org/w/index.php?title=File:Whampoa3.jpg *License*: Public Domain *Contributors*: Arilang1234, Hawyih, Olivier2, Stevenliuyi, 1 anonymous edits

Image:5062007131230.jpg *Source*: http://en.wikipedia.org/w/index.php?title=File:5062007131230.jpg *License*: Public Domain *Contributors*: Alexandrin, KTo288, Kaba, Severino666, Xhienne

Image:Ac.blyukher.jpg *Source*: http://en.wikipedia.org/w/index.php?title=File:Ac.blyukher.jpg *License*: unknown *Contributors*: Alex Bakharev, Ashtray, Hardscarf, Kl833x9, Mtsmallwood, Pauk

Image:Huangpu military school.jpg *Source*: http://en.wikipedia.org/w/index.php?title=File:Huangpu_military_school.jpg *License*: GNU Free Documentation License *Contributors*: User:BertholdD

Image:Whampoa-gate2.jpg *Source*: http://en.wikipedia.org/w/index.php?title=File:Whampoa-gate2.jpg *License*: Public Domain *Contributors*: Kl833x9, Olivier2, Uvo

Image:Kmtarmy.JPG *Source*: http://en.wikipedia.org/w/index.php?title=File:Kmtarmy.JPG *License*: Public Domain *Contributors*: Cchiang

Image:Chinesechildsoldier.jpg *Source*: http://en.wikipedia.org/w/index.php?title=File:Chinesechildsoldier.jpg *License*: Public Domain *Contributors*: US Army Signal Corps

Image:Countermand concession.jpg *Source*: http://en.wikipedia.org/w/index.php?title=File:Countermand_concession.jpg *License*: Public Domain *Contributors*: KTo288, Miborovsky, Millevache, Olivier2

Image:NRA marching and aircraft.jpg *Source*: http://en.wikipedia.org/w/index.php?title=File:NRA_marching_and_aircraft.jpg *License*: Public Domain *Contributors*: Arilang1234, Man vyi, Miborovsky, Sweeper tamonten

Image:Browning HP Inglis-2.jpg *Source*: http://en.wikipedia.org/w/index.php?title=File:Browning_HP_Inglis-2.jpg *License*: Attribution *Contributors*: M62, Nemo5576

Image:NRA cavalry.jpg *Source*: http://en.wikipedia.org/w/index.php?title=File:NRA_cavalry.jpg *License*: Public Domain *Contributors*: Miborovsky, Sweeper tamonten, Thib Phil, Wolfmann, 1 anonymous edits

Image:Menggukangriyoujidui.jpg *Source*: http://en.wikipedia.org/w/index.php?title=File:Menggukangriyoujidui.jpg *License*: Public Domain *Contributors*: Athaenara, SamOdin, Thib Phil, 1 anonymous edits

File:NRA machinegunners.jpg *Source*: http://en.wikipedia.org/w/index.php?title=File:NRA_machinegunners.jpg *License*: Public Domain *Contributors*: Avron, Harold, Miborovsky, Sweeper tamonten, 1 anonymous edits

file:Wuhan german divs.jpg *Source*: http://en.wikipedia.org/w/index.php?title=File:Wuhan_german_divs.jpg *License*: Public Domain *Contributors*: Artur Andrzej, Miborovsky, Sweeper tamonten, 1 anonymous edits

File:NRA march.jpg *Source*: http://en.wikipedia.org/w/index.php?title=File:NRA_march.jpg *License*: Public Domain *Contributors*: Avron, Homo lupus, JJ Georges, Mattes, Miborovsky, Millevache, Sweeper tamonten, 1 anonymous edits

File:Flag of Belgium (civil).svg *Source*: http://en.wikipedia.org/w/index.php?title=File:Flag_of_Belgium_(civil).svg *License*: Public Domain *Contributors*: Bean49, David Descamps, Dbenbenn, Denelson83, Evanc0912, Fry1989, Gabriel trzy, Howcome, Ms2ger, Nightstallion, Oreo Priest, Rocket000, Sir Iain, ThomasPusch, Warddr, Zscout370, 4 anonymous edits

File:Flag of Canada.svg *Source*: http://en.wikipedia.org/w/index.php?title=File:Flag_of_Canada.svg *License*: Public Domain *Contributors*: User:E Pluribus Anthony, User:Mzajac

File:Flag of Czechoslovakia.svg *Source*: http://en.wikipedia.org/w/index.php?title=File:Flag_of_Czechoslovakia.svg *License*: Public Domain *Contributors*: (of code)

File:Flag of Denmark.svg *Source*: http://en.wikipedia.org/w/index.php?title=File:Flag_of_Denmark.svg *License*: Public Domain *Contributors*: User:Madden

File:Flag of Italy (1861-1946).svg *Source*: http://en.wikipedia.org/w/index.php?title=File:Flag_of_Italy_(1861-1946).svg *License*: Creative Commons Attribution-Sharealike 2.5 *Contributors*: User:F l a n k e r

File:Flag of the Soviet Union.svg *Source*: http://en.wikipedia.org/w/index.php?title=File:Flag_of_the_Soviet_Union.svg *License*: Public Domain *Contributors*: A1, Ahmadi, Alex Smotrov, Alvis Jean, Art-top, BagnoHax, Denniss, ELeschev, Endless-tripper, EugeneZelenko, F l a n k e r, Fred J, Fry1989, G.dallorto, Garynysmon, Herbythyme, Homo lupus, Jake Wartenberg, MaggotMaster, Ms2ger, Nightstallion, Pianist, R-41, Rainforest tropicana, Sebyugez, Solbris, Storkk, Str4nd, Tabasco, ThomasPusch, Toben, Twilight Chill, Xgeorg, Zscout370, Серп, Тоны4, 55 anonymous edits

Image:1924 Emblem of Chinese Military Academy designed by Sun Yat-sen.gif *Source*: http://en.wikipedia.org/w/index.php?title=File:1924_Emblem_of_Chinese_Military_Academy_designed_by_Sun_Yat-sen.gif *License*: Public Domain *Contributors*: Sun Yat-sen

Image:WMD world map.svg *Source*: http://en.wikipedia.org/w/index.php?title=File:WMD_world_map.svg *License*: Creative Commons Attribution-Sharealike 2.5 *Contributors*: User:Andux, User:Fastfission, User:Simon, User:Vardion

File:Symbol book class2.svg *Source*: http://en.wikipedia.org/w/index.php?title=File:Symbol_book_class2.svg *License*: Creative Commons Attribution-Sharealike 2.5 *Contributors*: User:Lokal_Profil

File:Folder Hexagonal Icon.svg *Source*: http://en.wikipedia.org/w/index.php?title=File:Folder_Hexagonal_Icon.svg *License*: GNU Free Documentation License *Contributors*: User:John Cross, user:Shazz

File:Flag of the Republic of China.svg *Source*: http://en.wikipedia.org/w/index.php?title=File:Flag_of_the_Republic_of_China.svg *License*: Public Domain *Contributors*: 555, Bestalex, Bigmorr, Denelson83, Ed veg, Gzdavidwong, Herbythyme, Isletakee, Kakoui, Kallerna, Kibinsky, Mattes, Mizunoryu, Neq00, Nickpo, Nightstallion, Odder, Pymouss, R.O.C, Reisio, Reuvenk, Rkt2312, Rocket000, Runningfridgesrule, Samwingkit, Sasha Krotov, Shizhao, Tabasco, Vzb83, Wrightbus, ZooFari, Zscout370, 72 anonymous edits

Image:Shanghai 1932 military police.jpg *Source*: http://en.wikipedia.org/w/index.php?title=File:Shanghai_1932_military_police.jpg *License*: Public Domain *Contributors*: Davric, HongQiGong, Infrogmation, Miborovsky, Snlf1, 玄史生

Image:ROC military police.JPG *Source*: http://en.wikipedia.org/w/index.php?title=File:ROC_military_police.JPG *License*: Public Domain *Contributors*: User:Jiang

Image:T91-3 (65).JPG *Source*: http://en.wikipedia.org/w/index.php?title=File:T91-3_(65).JPG *License*: Attribution *Contributors*: SP Lee

Image:T75K1 by James Tung.JPG *Source*: http://en.wikipedia.org/w/index.php?title=File:T75K1_by_James_Tung.JPG *License*: Attribution *Contributors*: James Tung's Bulletin Board

Image:National_Martyrs_Shrine_(0732).JPG *Source*: http://en.wikipedia.org/w/index.php?title=File:National_Martyrs_Shrine_(0732).JPG *License*: Public Domain *Contributors*: User:Jiang

Image:Zhonglieci.jpg *Source*: http://en.wikipedia.org/w/index.php?title=File:Zhonglieci.jpg *License*: Creative Commons Attribution 3.0 *Contributors*: user:smartneddy

Image:Zhonglieci01.jpg *Source*: http://en.wikipedia.org/w/index.php?title=File:Zhonglieci01.jpg *License*: Creative Commons Attribution-Sharealike 3.0 *Contributors*: user:smartneddy

Image:National_Martyrs_Shrine_(0741).JPG *Source*: http://en.wikipedia.org/w/index.php?title=File:National_Martyrs_Shrine_(0741).JPG *License*: Public Domain *Contributors*: User:Jiang

File:Chang Chun Shrine amk.jpg *Source*: http://en.wikipedia.org/w/index.php?title=File:Chang_Chun_Shrine_amk.jpg *License*: Creative Commons Attribution-Sharealike 3.0 *Contributors*: User:AngMoKio

Image:Taiwan 2009 HuaLien Taroko Gorge FRD 5435 Pano Extracted.jpg *Source*: http://en.wikipedia.org/w/index.php?title=File:Taiwan_2009_HuaLien_Taroko_Gorge_FRD_5435_Pano_Extracted.jpg *License*: Creative Commons Attribution-Sharealike 3.0 *Contributors*: Fred Hsu (Wikipedia:User:Fred Hsu on en.wikipedia)

File:Armed_Forces_Muaeum_in_taipei.jpg *Source*: http://en.wikipedia.org/w/index.php?title=File:Armed_Forces_Muaeum_in_taipei.jpg *License*: Creative Commons Attribution-Sharealike 3.0 *Contributors*: Carpkazu

File:The_Order_of_National_Glory_Awarded_to_Chiang_Kai-Shek.jpg *Source*: http://en.wikipedia.org/w/index.php?title=File:The_Order_of_National_Glory_Awarded_to_Chiang_Kai-Shek.jpg *License*: Creative Commons Attribution-Sharealike 3.0 *Contributors*: User:Encyclopedist

CPSIA information can be obtained at www.ICGtesting.com
Printed in the USA
LVOW091728201212

312633LV00008B/487/P

9 781242 920950